Running Your Own Bed & Breakfast

Running Your Own Bed & Breakfast

Elizabeth Gundrey

PIATKUS

Copyright © 1989 by Elizabeth and Walter Gundrey

First published in Great Britain in 1989 by
Judy Piatkus (Publishers) Ltd of
5 Windmill Street, London W1

British Library Cataloguing in Publication Data

Gundrey, Elizabeth
    Running your own bed and breakfast.
    1. Bed & breakfast accommodation.
    Management
    I. Title
    647'.94'068

    ISBN 0-86188-800-6
    ISBN 0-86188-805-7 *Pbk*

Cover design by Paul Saunders
Jacket photograph by Andrew Lawson

Phototypeset in 11/12 Compugraphic Baskerville by
Action Typesetting Limited, Gloucester
Printed and bound in Great Britain by
Mackays of Chatham PLC

Contents

Contents

Acknowledgments

I am most grateful to the many proprietors whose generously shared experience and advice have contributed so greatly to *Running You Own B & B;* and in particular to Henry Howland (The Steppes, Herefordshire), Elizabeth and Geoffrey Griffin (Red House, Dorset), Malcolm Seymour (Somerset House, Avon), David Allen (Lansdowne House, Warwickshire), John London (The Orchard, Avon), Lynne Anderson (Coach House, Northumberland), Nicholas Hooper (Foxhill, Buckinghamshire), Norman Levitt (Trevena House, Surrey) and Pamela and Bill Kidd (Low Murrah, Cumbria).

I particularly wish to thank my brother Walter Gundrey not only for contributing, from his own practical experience of this subject, to the text of this book but also for his extensive comments and assistance when it was in manuscript.

I wish to thank the following owners for granting permission to reproduce the illustrations included in this book:

Miss M. Kempe, The Beehive, Dorset (title page), Mr and Mrs Jefferson, Orchard Guest House, Northumberland (page xiv), Mrs J. Lamb, Crosskeys, Norfolk (pages 4 and 9), Tregony House, Cornwall (page 32), Judy Seaborn, Stone House Farm, Hereford (page 51), Mr and Mrs Tilden, Penscot Farmhouse Hotel, Somerset (pages 75 and 106), Mrs Susan Trotman, White Barn, West Sussex (pages 141 and 170), Mrs Patricia Cooper, Long Candovers, Hampshire (page 168).

Publisher's Note

This book draws on the author's experiences of the bed and breakfast houses, farms, inns and small guest-houses featured in Elizabeth Gundrey's bestselling accommodation guide, *Staying Off the Beaten Track* (an annual Arrow paperback). For fuller information about them the reader is advised to obtain *Staying Off the Beaten Track* from bookshops, or by post for £7.75 from Explore Britain, Alston, Cumbria, CA9 3SL. As only houses inspected and recommended by Elizabeth Gundrey are included in the book, staying at some of them is a good way to study other people's bed and breakfast standards. When travelling abroad, too, seek out bed and breakfast accommodation for the useful experience it provides.

Where brand or company names are mentioned in the text, this means they have been recommended, but it does not necessarily mean they are the best ones to choose; shop around. When writing to any for details, please mention this book as your source of information.

References to laws relate to England; Scottish and other laws may differ.

Although all facts were checked before this book went to press, changes are constantly taking place, and the reader is advised to bear this in mind when taking decisions. Furthermore, opinions expressed are intended to stimulate thought rather than to be slavishly followed – for the world of bed and breakfast is full of individualists, each doing things their way; long may it remain so!

Introduction

This book is for anyone who takes, or plans to take, paying guests into their home, and aims at standards of excellence. This can mean anything from letting a single bedroom and providing breakfast only, through the letting of several rooms and offering an evening meal as well, to running a guest-house or private hotel where the provision of accommodation is the sole or main livelihood and the family occupies only a minor part of the house.

. More and more people are taking to this way of life. They include many newly retired people, particularly those to whom retirement comes early, as in the police force or the services, or is enforced through redundancy (with a redundancy payment providing necessary working capital). There are also those in steady jobs (some in the hotel and catering trade, many in other forms of management or executive work) who are tired of making money for other people and seek a way of achieving independence through self-employment. A number have longed for life in the country or by the sea, and offering bed and breakfast can make this move possible.

As a result, in England alone, there are over 14,000 bed and breakfast houses (over 3,000 are farms) registered with tourist boards – and thousands more not registered. Among the 24,000 registered 'hotels', there are thousands of small guesthouses and inns offering bed and breakfast.

Some people already have a home suited to this use. Keeping up a large house in the country is a costly matter when maintenance and heating bills run high; income from bed and breakfast can reduce the problem. Farmers having a lean time often find paying guests a profitable 'crop'. For mothers of young children, it is a job they can do without 'going out to work'; conversely, many older people have rooms and energy to spare once their children have grown up and left home. They – and widows or divorcees – may be glad of some company in the house as well as extra income, particularly if they can attract visitors who are congenial and appreciative of the home comforts that are offered. (If you provide only breakfast, however, you may lose the opportunity for real contact that dinner, or afterwards, supplies.)

And there are those who enjoy the exercise of the skills involved – cookery in particular – if evening meals are provided. Most people who enjoy, say, gardening or interior decorating like to share the results of their labours with visitors.

Some people are born hosts, or hostesses, and feel that the bed and breakfast life is just like having a perpetual house-party except that guests pay. Sometimes, however, people who provide bed and breakfast, though hardly aware of it themselves, are ambivalent about what they are doing, and like to keep up a pretence that they are simply receiving friends (until presenting the bill). This can lead to an uneasy situation, for the visitors are quite clear that they are paying for a service. They should never be made to feel that their host/hostess is condescending to allow them the 'privilege' of entering his/her home. On the contrary, the host/hostess is just as privileged to receive their custom.

A liking for people is, it goes without saying, the first essential for success. (Merely to see visitors as a source of money, not enjoyment, is a recipe for disaster; far better to earn a living from some impersonal activity.) New faces, some famous, and new events turn up daily; there is plenty of variety in this work.

Before deciding to venture into B & B, however, it is important to decide whether you are prepared for the following:

telephone calls (to book rooms) at all sorts of inconvenient hours; some arrivals late at night; some requests for very early breakfasts; the need to admit visitors even in the afternoon, which can be a nuisance in the case of innkeepers particularly; a diminution of your privacy (and your family's), with some restraints on behaviour – including your dog's;

difficulty in getting away for a day or a holiday, especially at
   peak seasons;

possible emergencies to be dealt with, from a guest's illness
   (even death) to your own, from plumbing mishaps to cooking
   ones – tiresome at any time but needing a good deal of cool-
   ness when the house is full of visitors;

acceptance of unmarried couples and homosexual couples;

the physical effort of bedmaking, cooking, and repeatedly
   helping to carry suitcases upstairs; how fit are your back and
   your legs?

the necessity to keep everywhere much tidier than perhaps you
   would normally do; an extra-heavy daily round of house-
   work; repainting and washing, cleaning, repairing or renewing furnishings more often;

a willingness to cater for guests' individual needs: some may be
   elderly or handicapped, on special diets (vegetarian, vegan,
   diabetic, etc.) or in need of travel advice (overseas visitors in
   particular);

patience and tact in the face of complaints (whether valid or
   not), inconsiderate behaviour, and occasional rudeness or
   dishonesty;

last but not least, a good deal of paperwork, official regulations
   to observe and record-keeping: far, far more than you may
   realise (see later chapters).

This list may sound formidable and, as one proprietor wrote,
'with the last guests of the year departing only yesterday I can
only confess to a state of almost total physical exhaustion. I
never appreciated the degree of commitment in time and energy
such an occupation would be.' But to be one's own boss, and to
work in one's own home, are two very great freedoms. A bed
and breakfast income (and tax benefits) that reduce your cost of
living may enable you to maintain a far better home and life-
style than would otherwise be the case: there are couples who
took to bed and breakfast simply to pay their children's school
fees, or to subsidise visits to relatives abroad. Many people
comment on the number of new friends they have made among
their guests – even to the point of receiving invitations to stay

with *them* in America, Australia, etc. And there is, finally, the satisfaction of a job well done when you say goodbye to visitors who, after arriving tired or stressed, depart with smiles and promises to return again. Running a bed and breakfast house should surely rank as one of the caring professions.

1.

Important Considerations

WHERE SHOULD YOU BUY YOUR PROPERTY?

Not every place is suitable for bed and breakfast trade; and not every place has a demand for accommodation all the year round. The first consideration is whether there are going to be enough visitors in your area to make the operation worthwhile.

Holiday areas

It is fairly obvious where most tourists want bed and breakfast (mainly in seaside resorts, though the Highlands, the Lake District, York and the Yorkshire Dales are almost as popular), but in such areas there may already be more bed and breakfast houses than the visitors can fill. You can check this by talking to staff at the nearest Tourist Information Centre. If local estate agents have a large number of guest-houses up for sale, it could be a bad sign. You might do better in some attractive but lesser known spot where there is not so much competition as in, say, Cornwall, Blackpool or Bournemouth, provided you can make your presence known (see chapter 8) to tourists as yet unaware of the charms of the area you have chosen. Bear in mind that many overseas (and other) tourists start from the south-east; those with limited time, or money for transport, will not go far.

Business travellers

People travelling on business also need accommodation within easy reach of where their business is. It is not only in cities that they may require a bed for the night. For example, a house in the Sussex countryside once built up a flourishing clientele of astronomers when nearby Herstmonceux Castle was an outpost of the Royal Observatory. One in Lincoln gets lawyers staying during the assizes, another gets archaeologists working at nearby Lewes, a house in Harrogate fills up with people attending the big conference centre there. There are others that benefit from being near a Channel ferry terminal or an airport. Houses near grouse moors are busy with shooting-parties during the game season. A West Country house gets entire groups of businessmen from Bristol because it is able to offer a small conference room too.

Proximity to a large boarding school can bring in visiting parents; courses in angling or some other sport can bring in residential students; a long-distance footpath will bring walkers; a pony-trekking centre, riders (a few country bed and breakfast houses find it possible to offer stabling for visitors' own horses); a nature reserve, birdwatchers; a marina, small boat owners; a motorway, travellers who want a break on a long journey.

Think of people whose work causes them to travel – school and factory inspectors, actors and musicians, surveyors, salesmen, TV film crews, judges on circuit – and think whether there is anything in the neighbourhood to bring them your way. If so, and provided you can make your presence known to them, you may secure regular business with steady repeat visits and, in some cases, lengthy stays. The salt baths at Droitwich bring visitors coming for spa treatment and they, too, need accommodation for a week or more. People who are house-hunting in an area distant from their home may need rooms while they search.

Local events

Another thing to consider is whether the local council is active in promoting tourism; or whether there are major annual events likely to bring you visitors: week-long regattas, for instance, or conferences or race meetings or arts festivals, the tulip fields of Lincolnshire or the apple-blossom trails of Kent, or music festivals in cathedral cities. Some local events, specialised but with an enthusiastic following, may create a wide demand: the south-west corner of the Lake District, outside the most popular area, fills up regularly for motorcycle events. These attractions are particularly valuable when they bring visitors at off-peak periods, and for more than just one night or two. Your local Tourist Information Centre is the best source of guidance on events that you may not have considered.

Highway or byway?

There are pros and cons to choosing whether to be on a main road. If your house is on one, it is easy to bring in visitors by putting up a bed and breakfast sign, but not everyone wants to do this. It means you have no control over who is going to turn up, or when; nor will you have advance warning of their arrival. On the other hand, you can have a quick look at them and, if you do not like what you see, say you have no vacancies. If you do put up such a sign, design it so that you can add a 'no vacancies' board when you wish, in order to save yourself – and the traveller – the annoyance of pointless calls.

Many people want to get away from traffic, and a less exposed position may be preferable even though you will have to work harder at getting your presence known and spend more on advertising.

Either way, to have a railway station or coach stop within reach is an asset, since not everybody has access to a car (and overseas visitors often rely on public transport). If you are willing to meet trains or coaches, or to go to airports in your car, say so in your brochure (no great effort if combined with shopping); and keep rail, coach and bus timetables. Proximity to an inn or restaurant can be a help, particularly if you do bed and breakfast only, as visitors to these may then come to you for accommodation.

Demand in the area

Look at other bed and breakfast operations nearby (stay at some), obtain their brochures, and notice the kind of visitors they are getting (the sort of cars parked outside may be a guide) and whether there are many 'no vacancies' signs up. Are they open all year or not? Obtain (free) a 'Tourism Regional Fact Sheet' from the regional Tourist Board which will tell you a lot about tourists reaching the area, and ask also for the region's 'Tourism Strategy' detailing its future plans. Make enquiries at the local Chamber of Commerce or tourism association about the need for more bed and breakfast provision in the area, and at the County Council's economic development office about plans for years to come.

The holiday season

Bed and breakfast trade is apt to fluctuate with the seasons, unless you are in a town that attracts year-round travellers needing a bed for the night. Obviously, tourism peaks in summer as a rule, but there is a tendency now for many people to take short breaks in spring and autumn too. Sea-and-sand resorts are the most highly seasonal (unlike, say, the Lake District, which at any time attracts more walkers than sun-bathers) and at seaside resorts trade can drop disastrously if a summer is cold or wet.

July and August remain peak months for families whose movements are dictated by school holidays; but these are not peak periods in, for instance, Brighton, which is now less of a resort than a conference centre; and older couples tend to avoid July-August in favour of less crowded months. (Such factors will influence how you plan your house: whether to provide family rooms, for example, or twin beds, which are often preferred by the elderly.)

Special events such as races, festivals, etc. create local peaks. Only local enquiry and a few years' experience will tell you what occupancy rate you can expect; (that is, how many of your beds will be occupied each week) and if there is a run of bad summers the figures may be disappointing. Financial planning should allow for this contingency.

Winter opening

At some bed and breakfast houses, charges go up and down according to the month – raised in midsummer to exploit demand, lowered in winter in the hope of enticing visitors. At a few houses, rates go *up* in winter to cover the extra cost of heating, for this is a major consideration (in 1988 it was estimated at 50p minimum per room per night). Some people close in winter to save on heating bills. Others very unwisely stay open but skimp on heating: a regular cause of complaint is cold rooms in winter, particularly from southern visitors when travelling north (though my own worst experience was in

Cornwall one unexpectedly cold January: hard winters are un-usual there, so houses are not always equipped with the same amount of heating and double-glazing as in the north). It is bad for the upkeep of a house to leave a number of rooms unheated all through the winter, or to heat them intermittently: problems of condensation, mildew or frozen pipes may result. It is never very successful to try to heat up rooms only when a visitor is due. If you intend to open in winter, take into account the cost of providing any portable heaters, electric blankets, etc. which visitors may expect to be available; and remember that insur-ance premiums may be reduced for periods when you are closed to visitors, so you will lose that benefit too.

Another consideration about when to stay open is your own wellbeing, particularly if you are coping without any staff. You need not only a proper holiday but other days off too. It is important to be able to set certain periods aside for your own relaxation, whether in the winter or at other seasons. A closed period is also useful for redecoration and repairs, for making improvements such as installing washbasins or additional bath-rooms, and for stocking your larder (and your freezer, with part-prepared meals).

Depending on local demand, you *may* be able to operate for fewer than seven days a week, but this is usually hard to achieve. Certainly it is feasible to offer dinner on only certain evenings in the week (specified in advance).

If you care to cater for it, there is a definite demand now for Christmas accommodation – not necessarily with any special Christmas meals (some people want to get away from all that) or, indeed, with any meals at all – some of the demand will be from people who want to visit, but not stay with, relatives. As in so much of the bed and breakfast scene, there are no firm rules, and each person works out his/her own plan, to suit his/her own needs and in the light of what demand there is locally.

If you decide to stay open throughout winter, it goes without saying that the house should be open to visitors in the afternoon if bad weather forces them to return early from sightseeing: indeed, after October, darkness begins to fall early. Provision of electric blankets, hot-water bottles, extra blankets, and hot drinks at bedtime are all little touches worth offering (particularly for older visitors); the extra running costs and trouble are minimal, and they will be greatly appreciated.

One thing which always produces exclamations of pleasure (and not only in cold weather) is a crackling fire: a real treat for city-dwellers who never experience this at home. Another is a glass sun-room or conservatory which, if south-facing, is likely to get very warm even in winter.

Something else to consider is the indoor entertainment of visitors. Many may be content with a good book by the fire or in bed – but only if you have provided adequate lighting. One of the most common errors of omission I have found is inadequate light for reading in bed. The same applies in sitting-rooms: small wall-lamps and central ceiling lights are totally ineffective for this purpose. The consumption of electricity for lighting is negligible, so you might just as well do the job properly, as what is at stake is your visitors' satisfaction with their visit to your house.

Visitors forced indoors by bad weather will nevertheless not feel their stay was a total loss if the house itself provides diversions to pass the time. Well stocked bookshelves and a record player are two obvious examples. Increasingly, video-recorders are being provided, not only with a stock of video films but also in order to allow guests to record daytime programmes (e.g. sports events) for viewing when they come in later. If you have space for a games-room, think about such pursuits as snooker, table-tennis and darts. A fitness room can be equipped with sauna, Jacuzzi, exercise cycle, sunbed, etc., but at considerable cost. Very little expense is needed to provide a supply of table games: chess, draughts, Trivial Pursuit, Scrabble, backgammon and so on, as well as cards and a folding card-table for bridge-players.

Keep a 'wet weather file' of local sights, leisure centres, museums, etc. which are under cover, particularly those that stay open during winter; and make available the local newspaper for details of what is on at the cinema, theatre, etc., as well as TV programmes. It is well worth writing out a list of recommended car tours enjoyable even in wet weather.

Winter is the season during which to lay on speciality

weekends in your house if you think these would attract your summer holidaymakers to return for an out-of-season break. (For instance: cookery or craft demonstrations, a gourmet or a curry weekend, music weekends, wine-tastings, talks on collecting antiques, painting tuition, birdwatching – see chapter 11.) What you can offer will depend upon your own talents and interests, or those of local people you could involve. This kind of venture may be one to launch in co-operation with one or two other guest houses in your vicinity for guest numbers to justify running it, but even with only three bedrooms, one in Cornwall finds it worthwhile to run cookery courses in the kitchen.

It is worth emphasising in your brochure such off-peak attractions as your log fires or undercover swimming pool, as well as the area's autumn colours (New Forest), illuminations (Blackpool), veteran car rally (Brighton), and all kinds of pre-Christmas events including shopping and special attractions in theatres and cathedrals everywhere; and to enquire what off-peak publicity your regional Tourist Board can get for you (many issue *Let's go* booklets on off-peak breaks).

The British Tourist Authority encourages autumn and winter opening through its 'How to Succeed in Off-Peak Marketing' – a regular bulletin worth getting for the ideas which it contains: free from BTA, Thames Tower, London W6 9EL, together with a *Guide to Off Peak Marketing*. Among much useful information, this invaluable guide points out that older people whose families have grown up are particularly inclined to travel in quieter off-peak periods; and so, for different reasons, are young people (under 30) who are attracted to the winter entertainments of big resorts or cities, and who do not have school-age children yet. The guide lists 50 things you can do to attract such off-peak visitors to your house.

The peak periods for short breaks (mainly weekends) are not summer but spring and September in most places; and December, in and around London and in the West Midlands. It is easier to attract winter visitors (particularly from Europe, where there are a number of public holidays in the winter) in the south-east than in the north, and inland rather than on the coast. Some bed and breakfast houses have tried – at slack periods – to supplement their normal trade with handicapped or homeless people whose payments are made by the Department of Health and Social Security. If you want to explore this possibility, enquire at your local council. Check whether payment can be made direct to you by the DHSS or, if not, what assurance you have of actually getting it.

2.
What Will Your Visitors Need?

It will be obvious, by now, that there is a variety of factors which may bring travellers to your house. The guests will be old and young, fit and infirm, singles and families, and people from all over the world (Britain gets nearly two million overseas visitors a year – though these are outnumbered four-to-one by British travellers).

Some may stay with you for a week or two (particularly if your house is by the seaside) but many for only a day or two because the car has made people so mobile that touring has largely replaced the stay-put holiday of the past. On the other hand, there may be a demand for long-term bookings (for example, from students) which you may or may not want.

Sometimes people who come in one capacity return in another. The owner of a farm in Oxfordshire has many RAF personnel staying during the winter months because there are two signals units down the road. Every year several of these men come back with their families for a holiday, because they have looked through the information folders in their rooms telling them about what is to be seen in the area.

To some extent you can regulate the type of people you get – by carefully selecting the media in which you publicise yourself (see later chapter), and by the way you describe the house in your brochure, by its exterior appearance, and by prices; all these establish what kind of place you run and help to ensure you get the kind of visitors that suit it.

In Brixham a notice on one house says 'no divers', while up in the north another house goes out of its way to cater for divers (with a special room for their gear, drying facilities, etc.). If you want walkers, anglers, etc., think about their particular needs. Both may be glad of facilities for drying clothes and boots, and of packed lunches; the latter may need to make a 6 a.m. start, and freezer-space for their catch.

As regards other people with special needs, it is important to decide at the outset whether or not you want to cater for them (and to make this clear in your brochure).

Businessmen

Often businessmen are prepared to pay more than holiday-makers, but they tend to demand more too – arriving late, leaving early, and making heavy use of the telephone. They usually need rooms only on Monday to Thursday nights. If you want to encourage them, it is a good idea to equip bedrooms with a writing-table and desk lamp, trouser-press and radio-alarm – none of this extra expense would be necessary for holidaymakers. Businessmen more than other tourists appreciate a bar or, failing that, will probably want to bring their own drinks. If you want to specialise in business visitors, study the local Yellow Pages and send your brochure to selected firms in your area (write to the managing directors' secretaries).

Putting a direct-dial telephone into each bedroom is an expensive business. If there is no telephone kiosk close to your house, you can rent a payphone, to put in the hall or somewhere more private, or one incorporating a 'telemeter' which not only times calls but indicates their cost: however, neither is cheap. If, as an alternative, you ask guests to use the ADC system ('advice of duration and charge') and then repay you, or to have charges transferred to the recipient of the call, remember that neither service is free.

Where incoming calls are concerned, one expedient is to have, as an extension to your own telephone, a cordless phone on the landing which the recipient of the call can take into his or her own bedroom to use (with a security button to prevent outgoing calls).

In many houses, the best compromise may be to install a

Monitel. This electrical device monitors not only the time each call takes but also its cost (the user presses a button to indicate the rate of charge, as given in the Dialling Codes book). The user then writes down the sum shown at the end of the call, to be added to his/her bill when he/she leaves: one model actually delivers a ticket with the amount on it. Given that most people are honest, this is an excellent system.

Dog-owners

Dog-owners (27% of the UK population) have difficulty in finding hotels willing to accept pets, so you will be much in demand if you are prepared to take them (you could advertise in the *Pets Welcome* directory), though you may lose those visitors who dislike dogs or are allergic to them. But there are other reasons for hesitating, not least the fact that, according to a recent Gallup survey, one dog in eight is accustomed to sleeping on its owner's bed (even more in Wales!).

Many people who run bed and breakfast houses refuse to allow dogs in the dining- or sitting-rooms, for the sake of other guests. Conversely, some owners will allow them in the downstairs sitting-room but not in the bedrooms because of the hairs and smell they may leave behind.

A common compromise is to require dogs to sleep in the car but allow them in the house except at mealtimes. But if you insist it must sleep in its owner's car, a dog may bark all night or at unusual sounds (or be teased by roving vandals if in an urban area). At the very least, keep a dog-basket available or insist that owners bring one. A dog left alone in a strange bedroom during mealtimes may panic and, in an effort to get out, damage furnishings and woodwork, or get on the (possibly non-washable) bedspread.

Your policy will probably be dictated by your own attitude to dogs: some owners refuse them because they have none and don't like them – some because they like them and have enough of their own!

If you allow one visitor's dog (dogs, indeed), you are obliged to allow others' and the result may be pandemonium. Normally mild dogs often behave out of character in strange surroundings. If you have a dog of your own, consider how it will react. At a Cotswold inn, a lady who enquired by telephone about dogs was told that they were accepted if not too large. Reply: only two little Cairns. On the day, the visitors arrived with two Cairns, two Alsatians, and an Old English Sheepdog!

You may find that an unfortunate experience forces you to change your policy: a Cumbrian proprietor stopped taking dogs after one of her private baths was scratched by two spaniels being bathed in it (and her carpet was soaked). This was hardly the dogs' fault, and the moral is that you have to size up the owners' standards of house-training as well as their dogs'.

As to your own pets, the owner of a Northumberland guesthouse, who likes dogs, has this to say: 'As host, cast an eye over them and ensure that they are fit for polite society. It is quite wrong to submit your guests to a trial by Fido. Your dogs must be of unimpeachable temperament if they are to mix with your guests. They should also be kept clean and well groomed.' To this I would add that there are few things more unwelcoming than a dog barking at you as soon as the front door opens, or sniffing up your legs, or finding the best armchair occupied by a dog – particularly if it is in need of a bath.

However, dogs can be an asset, as many guests like them.

Of course, dogs are not the only pets people may want to bring along: you might, like one proprietor, find yourself playing host to a goat!

Single visitors

In an attempt to make as much money as possible, some people try to turn even the smallest bedrooms into doubles (with very cramped results); but there is a substantial demand for single rooms in some areas, particularly from businessmen, students, and the large number of widows in our population; even when two travel together, they usually do not want to share a room. (Half the over-60s in Britain are single). Also, people sometimes travel in threesomes, such as a couple with one in-law or a grown-up son or daughter.

An American Express survey found that 30% of holiday-makers are single, so if you can provide a single room or two, and publicise the fact, it is likely to be in demand. As a compromise, a room which would make a large single but not an adequate double might be provided with an extra folding bed or cot to take two children on occasion.

At some houses, singles are charged far more than half a double booking whether they get a single room or the use of a double one, which seems grossly unfair. At the very least, a single should be acceptable (and at a reasonable price) when the booking is made at short notice and a double room might otherwise stand empty. But beware the single who smuggles in a partner after dark.

Single women travelling on business often prefer a friendly bed and breakfast house to a big commercial hotel in which they feel conspicuous and lonely, are given the worst tables, and may be treated offensively in the bar.

Bed and breakfast owners should see an opportunity in single visitors: here is a growing market well worth cultivating, and you can offer something with which the big fish in the hotel trade cannot compete, for just talking to a solitary traveller and making him or her feel welcome and at home costs nothing and is worth far more than the expensive show of large hotels.

Single travellers might appreciate dining at a shared table rather than separate ones, and the chance to meet other guests over a pre-dinner drink or after-dinner coffee in the sitting-room; but some might prefer their own company, so do check.

Visitors on special diets or with allergies

Your brochure should, particularly if you offer evening meals, make it clear whether you are prepared to provide food for special needs. There is an increasing number of vegetarians now and it is not good enough to offer merely an omelette or cauliflower cheese. Check whether your vegetarian guest eats fish; or is a vegan: if so, he or she will eat no eggs or dairy products as well as meat. And remember the 'hidden' animal content in, say, mincemeat or prepared puff-pastry. Many people, too, want low-fat, low calorie or other healthier meals: for them, it is a good idea to have available wholemeal bread, alternatives to butter (such as Flora), muesli or bran cereals, decaffeinated coffee, unrefined sugar and artificial sweeteners. If you can say that you use organic produce, free-range eggs and wholefood recipes, this will be a big attraction to many visitors. Muslim and Jewish people will not eat any pork products, offal or shellfish. In addition, you will occasionally be asked to cater for very special diets: diabetic (easy), coeliac (difficult), etc. If you are prepared to try, ask the visitor to send you notes on his or her requirements beforehand. Useful free leaflets on various special diets are published by Sainsburys (obtainable by post from their Customer Relations Department, Stamford House, London SE1).

Your own convictions (in the case of organic and vegetarian catering) or experience (in the case of more clinical diets) is probably the best reason for offering to fill these needs. If you do so, there are specialised publications through which you will be able to make your house known.

Another special requirement you may need to take into account is allergies. Some people are allergic to feather and down pillows or duvets; or dogs, cats or birds.

Overseas visitors

These will inevitably come your way, and many people particularly enjoy the experience of having guests from other cultures who are widely travelled. What a pity that so few trouble to use even the rudiments of foreign languages to greet their guests!

Be prepared for some unfamiliar habits and requirements. Some Americans are often very concerned about hygiene and the necessity for en suite bathrooms (what they really mean is the lavatory). They will expect you to provide a face-cloth, are often unfamiliar with egg-cups (they break their eggs onto the plate), think 'pudding' means 'blancmange' and 'inn' any kind of accommodation, wash their hair daily (and so need hair-dryers), and dislike hot-water bottles – 'There's a horrible thing in my bed!' screamed one lady, rushing terrified down-stairs in her nightie. They call duvets 'comforters', and our 'first' floor is their 'second'. They appear to eat smaller portions (steaks excepted) than the British and may well follow unusual diets.

In America, Frommer publish many where-to-stay guides with worldwide coverage. (One includes advice to people running bed and breakfast houses in America, and I was interested to read what hosts there provide – such as vacuum flasks of coffee placed outside the bedroom door early each morning, 'picnic basket' breakfasts in bed, carafes of iced water placed by the bedside each night.)

You will hear much prejudiced talk about other nationalities, but as soon as you have heard how rude French children are you will hear from someone else how well behaved they are. Some find Americans a nuisance (booking and not turning up, for instance, is a frequent complaint); others sing their praises.

One thing is very clear since the Libyan crisis caused Americans to cancel in droves for fear of reprisals on Britain: do not rejoice if you get a high proportion of your trade from this quarter, because it can be a very fickle market. Not only terrorist scares but pound/dollar fluctuations can change it overnight. (The British may not be such big spenders, but on the whole they are more dependable: a point to remember when deciding what to charge.) It is not anti-American prejudice which causes some proprietors to limit American bookings to 50% of their rooms at any one time. Moreover, Americans come here to meet the British, not just one another.

Incidentally, if an Australian tells you he doesn't want any *snags* for breakfast, all he means is that he doesn't like sausages!

With all overseas visitors, be prepared to help them with travel information, instruction on our currency and how to use telephones, and shopping and car-driving advice. It would be a kindness to stock road maps to sell to them: they rarely arrive properly equipped with these. You may need to provide an adaptor for (e.g.) shavers.

Foreign students (child or adult) come in vast numbers to some areas, staying a couple of weeks or up to three months to learn English. Their colleges pay their bills; but problems of communication and keeping order will be largely left to you if you accommodate them (so it is vital to know where to reach their organiser if need arises). A list of such colleges and a leaflet, *A Foreign Student in Your Home,* are obtainable from the Association of Recognised English Language Schools (2 Pontypool Place, Valentine Place, London SE1 8QF), which also knows about accommodation agencies specialising in this kind of visitor travelling individually. You will usually be expected to provide meals, talk (in English), and generally befriend the student – for which services you may reasonably charge more than your usual bed and breakfast rate. A student will need a desk and quiet. As the room will be heavily used (as a bedsitter), it may be wise to have a washable bedspread, glass over any polished tabletop, and good lighting. Some overseas students need to be told about the use of British baths, lavatories and sanibins; and the Highway Code (if they have a car or bicycle). There are special regulations regarding students under 16. All this and much else is covered in the leaflet mentioned above.

Children

From the start, a clear policy is needed on whether you are going to accept children or not. If you do, it may lose you some visitors who want peace and quiet. A compromise is to accept children only during, say, Easter and summer holidays. Houses which normally do not take children may find their rooms vacant then, because people without children mistakenly think this is a crowded period, better avoided. If this is your experience, it may be a good idea to state in your brochure that families *with* children are accepted in July and August only.

It may be unwise to take small children if your premises have hazards such as a deep pool or nearby traffic. Will your own children like or dislike strange children on 'their' territory?

Many people specify a minimum age in order to exclude certain categories: for instance, the under-fives, because crying may disturb other guests, there are possible problems over nappies and feeding-bottles, and a cot and high chair will usually be needed. Others are quite happy to take babies, and offer the use of a washing-machine and to baby-sit. (In this context, it is worth mentioning a useful and moderately priced device called the *Bug Plug:* plugged into a socket near the baby, it will relay any sound to another plug inserted elsewhere in the house or outdoors where you, or your visitors, are sitting.)

Others say they do not want any child under 12 or so, regarding younger children of this age group as a noisy and active group likely to disturb other visitors, damage furnishings, and (at a shared dining-table) inhibit conversation. Those who do accommodate young children are often prepared to offer 'nursery teas' earlier than the parents' dinner, and to provide indoor and outdoor games for the children.

Babies are sometimes accepted free or for a nominal charge if they come in a carry-cot and do not require meals, even though their needs may make heavy demands on the hot-water supply, and the mother may be in and out of the kitchen to heat feeds or to use the liquidiser.

Children accommodated in parents' rooms are normally charged less than adults (or may even be charged only for meals). Where bedwetting is a risk, (even normally dry children sometimes bedwet when in strange surroundings), it is wise to have a waterproof mattress-cover available , but with an under-blanket between it and the sheet (otherwise it is slippery and clammy to sleep on).

A large double room becomes a family room if a single bed or a pair of bunks is added: less obtrusive alternatives are sofa-beds, Z-beds (which fold up and can be taken away when not needed), Wentle beds which fold up into a cupboard, or a pair of single beds where one slides below the other when not required. There are a number of ingenious ways to make double rooms serve as family rooms without turning the place into a dormitory: the creation of a curtained alcove, for example, or one enclosed by louvred shutters; and, in high rooms, the building of a gallery above and behind the parents' bed, reached by a safely secured ladder – suitable for older children. Often a room unsuitable for adults is ideal for children: a low-ceilinged attic is an example. L-shaped rooms are ideal for families as, like alcoves or galleries, they can provide an element of privacy for the parents.

Those who do choose to take children and to make them really welcome are likely to find a big response, for such places are not very easy to find. A farm in Devon won the AA's 'farm of the year' award in 1981 because it excelled in this way; even more convincing are the scores of letters and drawings from child guests which line one wall of the sitting-room there. Children are taken on hay-rides or pony-rides round the farm, there are table-tennis and badminton in an outhouse, a nature trail round the grounds has been marked out (with a quiz), and indoors are table-skittles and other games for wet days.

Children should not be a nuisance if there is plenty for them to do: books, toys, board games and even dressing-up clothes are easy to provide. A separate playroom (in cellar, attic or out-house) is ideal, as is a separate play area in the garden with things like swings and slides.

If you want to attract families to an area that is not as obviously interesting to children as the seaside, it is worth listing for parents all the local possibilities: you may surprise yourself when you call at the local Tourist Information Centre for advice. For instance, the town of Cirencester, in Gloucestershire, is not an obvious choice for a holiday with children, but after an article I wrote about it in *Parents* magazine an inn there was inundated with bookings because I listed a dozen things for a family to do and see in the neighbourhood: horse-drawn carriage rides, feeding fish at Prinknash Abbey, picnicking in the gardens of Westbury, steam railway, toy museum, flying falcons, bird gardens, stream suitable for paddling, chicks hatching at a rare breeds farm, wildlife park, butterfly farm, and the house of Beatrix Potter's 'Tailor of Gloucester' (with playroom). And there are practical ways, too, in which you can tempt families to choose your house, some (like the use of a washing-machine) already mentioned, or the offer of kitchen facilities where parents can prepare early meals for children, thus saving money as well as providing a convenience.

If you do decide to go to town on providing for children, make this known in your brochure and by telling the editorial department of specialist magazines (*Parents, Nursery World,* etc.)

which may pass the good news on to their readers. There are also accommodation directories in which you might get a listing: *Children Welcome* and the *Family Welcome Guide,* for instance.

This also applies to any other special group mentioned in this book. There are numerous magazines for walkers, anglers, riders, the disabled, dog-owners, vegetarians, slimmers, overseas visitors … a glance through the magazine shelves of any big newsagent will give you ideas and your local reference library will be able to produce addresses of more, and of clubs and associations with relevant memberships (dog-owners, disabled, diabetics or whatever). See also Chapter 7.

Disabled people

'Disability' covers a multitude of conditions, from almost total immobility to difficulty in climbing stairs. Since advancing years is a common cause of disability, the proportion of handicapped people in the population is high (for 30% of the population is over 55) and increasing. So to make provision for them is not just considerate but good business sense: over-60s, it has been found, spend about 30% more on their holidays than younger people do. (Not surprising, when you realise that two-thirds of all private savings belong to this age-group.) And when you consider that, by making it possible for one handicapped person to stay with you, you may be securing the custom of a whole family whose choice of holiday is dictated by the requirements of one disabled member, the advantages of providing facilities for the disabled become even more apparent.

How far to go in making provision for the wide range of disability depends on your own inclinations and the potential of your property. Some houses require little or no adaptation, and though older ones may be disqualified by steep, narrow stairs and changes of floor level, this is not always so. (There is an extremely ancient Yorkshire farmhouse where the owner herself is disabled and has installed a stairlift for her own use.) Nor do you have to make every room suitable for every degree of disability.

Your house will be a possibility for visitors with a minor

degree of handicap, such as an artificial leg or a weak heart, if it has most of the following: wide, shallow stairs with few bends; downstairs bedroom, bathroom and lavatory, or a lift; and level access from outside.

Complete mobility for wheelchair users demands more:

a wide parking space;
a ramp (perhaps a moveable wooden one) to the front door;
no changes of level, twisting corridors, etc. between bedrooms
    and public rooms;
all doors at least 30″ wide;
minimum space of 48″ beside both the bed and the lavatory;
bedroom and bathroom big enough for a wheelchair user to
    turn inside and to close the door;
grab rails by bath, lavatory and shower.

Before you embark on alterations, expert advice is necessary. A proprietor who has much experience in this field suggests that you contact the physiotherapy department of your local hospital. They should be able to arrange a visit by a DHSS engineer trained to alter and equip existing premises for disabled guests.

The British Tourist Authority (Thames Tower, London W6 9EL) publishes *Catering for the Disabled*. The other main sources of advice are RADAR (the Royal Association for Disability and Rehabilitation) and the Disabled Living Foundation. These and other national organisations are listed inside the back cover of the Yellow Pages directory, inside which you should also find details of local branches of such bodies as the Multiple Sclerosis Society, the Spinal Injuries Association, the Polio Fellowship, and the Red Cross. The Holiday Care Service (2 Old Bank Chambers, Horley, Surrey, RH6 9HW) has a free booklet called *Providing for Disabled Visitors*.

Some of these will give advice on the suitability of your premises for their members and on adaptations, and many will help you to publicise your house among the disabled community through lists of accommodation they keep, newsletters they issue, and so on. RADAR publishes a 'Holiday Fact Sheet', which lists many associations worth telling about your accommodation, and also the annual *Holidays for Disabled People*, in which you might be listed. The AA (Fanum House, Basingstoke, RG21 2EA) publishes a *Guide for the Disabled*.

Some organisations may point you towards sources of grants for conversion work, which may also be obtainable from your regional Tourist Board. If yours is a country house, you may be able to get a grant from the Country Landowners' Charitable Trust (Bohune Common House, Woodborough, Wilts, SN9 6LY). Grants are also available from it to provide country recreational facilities in your grounds for wheelchair users, such as nature trails or platforms for angling.

Your local branch of the Royal Institute of British Architects may have among its members architects specialising in designing for the disabled. Otherwise, do not rely on your builder or architect knowing how such work should be done. Advice from a nurse, a disabled friend, or best of all a physiotherapist will be more useful.

If you have your own experience to guide you, so much the better: once a teacher of handicapped children, the owner of a Yorkshire guest-house has added a special extension for the disabled whose needs she knows well. It includes sitz baths and an emergency bell.

There is no need to go to extremes. One or two suitable or adapted rooms may suffice, and all that is required may be just a little extra thought given to the position of a lavatory or the size of a doorway when you are planning alterations or extensions. It is pointless and very expensive to indulge in lots of equipment and rails which will obstruct the path of many disabled people and may be aesthetically offensive to your other guests.

The nuts and bolts of adaptation are not all: little extras you may dream up – like some half-height hanging space so that a paraplegic guest can hang up his or her own jacket, and seating wheelchair-bound guests at a refectory table, not one with legs – will show you really care, and ensure repeat visits.

You could have on hand for such visitors the National Trust's booklet *Facilities for Disabled and Visually Handicapped Visitors* (free from 36 Queen Anne's Gate, London SW1H 9AB for a stamped addressed sticky label) to help them with outings; and the particulars of the nearest Hertz branch which can provide one of their hand-controlled hire-cars.

Above all, when disabled guests are using the rooms, there must be adequate heating, and you must be prepared for it to be on higher and for more hours a day than for other guests.

In the case of the blind you could relax a no-dogs rule.

Except in specialist publications, it is probably inadvisable to publicise the fact that your accommodation has been modified with the disabled in mind: other people may get the mistaken idea that the result must be clinical or institutional. But, catering for disabled people can be rewarding financially and personally, and work undertaken on their behalf can upgrade accommodation for all your guests.

Smokers

An increasing number of houses are designating themselves 'no smoking', while at others smoking is prohibited in some parts: in bedrooms (where it is a fire risk, as well as leaving furnishings smelly for the next visitor), at table and/or in the sitting-room. Some owners are able to set aside a second sitting-room for smokers; or allow smoking in one bedroom only (but that involves questioning the visitor at the time of booking). Fear of losing trade is unfounded, as smokers now generally accept restrictions, while those who strongly dislike the smell are attracted to 'no smoking' houses. A compromise is to install electric air purifiers that get ride of smoke.

A survey among hotels carried out by the magazine *Caterer & Hotelkeeper* found that 'no smoking' policies were proving successful and that side benefits include the reduced need for frequent redecoration, no ashtrays to empty, and no burn marks.

Do not provide ashtrays if you do not want smoking. Small notices discouraging it are available free from the British Heart Foundation at 102 Gloucester Place, London W1. (If you do allow it, be sure wastepaper bins and sanitary bins are of non-flammable metal.)

Troublesome visitors

In general, the better your own standards, the better the visitors you will get. Cheap and nasty boarding-houses are the ones that tend to get people who pinch the towels, let baths overflow and leave without paying. There are exceptions, of course, and talking to owners of bed and breakfast houses suggests that there are some ways of spotting troublesome guests, such as the born complainers, before you accept them. The kind of person who telephones inconsiderately late; whose *first* question is about the price; who chops and changes over what he/she wants and when; who is overbearing or petulant even when making an initial enquiry; who pleads with you to waive any rules you have, such as no dogs or the times of meals – these are the kinds of people whom you may regret accepting. Others to beware of are those who ask for facilities your brochure shows you do not have, such as private bathrooms; who demur at sending you written confirmation with a deposit; or who decline to give their address and telephone number. You are entirely free, in law, to say no to anyone you do not want in your home – only an inn is under an obligation to accept all comers.

But tiresome visitors are very much the exception, and most give their hosts much pleasure by their appreciation of what is provided. One proprietor has said: 'I feel that if I stay here long enough most of the interesting people in the world will pass through my dining-room – this year we had air commodores and actresses, artists and archbishops, secretaries to royals and a NATO general; publishers, international horse-riders, orienteers and a large party of ornithologists. Indonesians and Coptic Christians from Bengal, a Swiss art dealer and a Polish family, Anglican vicars and Israeli paratroopers, Scandinavians, Belgians, antipodean wanderers – the conversation between them is fascinating. One American, an irrigation expert with the World Health Organisation, spent an evening being educated in the finer points of cricket by a prep school headmaster and a Group Captain of the Queen's Flight – I think it was possibly the high spot of his whole trip!'

24

3.

The House

Perhaps you are already living in a house suitable for bed and breakfast visitors or one which, with alterations, could be made so. But more is needed than just a spare bedroom or two. Whether you are intending to move or not, questions to ask yourself are the following.

Lavatories and baths.
Have you sufficient for the family plus the maximum number of visitors? Is the hot water system able to cope at peak periods of demand? If not, can you find space for additions? (It is not a good idea to expect visitors to use a bathroom littered with the family's gear; and one lavatory to about eight people is an absolute minimum, and then only if it is not in the bathroom.) If more than one family share a bathroom, it should be checked before each arrival.

Dining- and sitting-rooms.
Even if only breakfast is served, guests will need somewhere to sit in the evening, unless their bedrooms are so spacious that you can equip them with really comfortable armchairs. In summer, a garden with chairs is an asset. (In a few bed and breakfast houses, breakfast is served in bedrooms, and no other rooms are available, in which case a table with chairs is necessary.)

Family privacy.
Can your own part of the house be kept sufficiently separate? If you do not intend to dine with your guests, where will you eat, and sit after dinner?

25

Extensions.

Is there space for these, and will you be able to get planning permission? Sometimes adding a large conservatory with dining-tables or armchairs is a solution, particularly in an historic house which modern brickwork might ruin. (One proprietor believes that adding a conservatory quadrupled his bar sales.) Aluminium frames – white or bronze – need no painting, window-cleaning is not expensive, double-glazing keeps warmth in and roof blinds provide shade on hot days, and guests may enjoy the view out. Occasionally I have come across people who, needing more income than they are getting from their few bedrooms, think of building more. But if the existing rooms are not fully occupied it would be better to spend money and effort improving the occupancy rate of these. Many running costs of a house are much the same whether it is half or fully occupied; so every extra bed-night achieved is almost wholly profit. Building an extension, however, will entail greater running costs (as well as capital expenditure) with no guarantee that the rooms will be filled.

Buying a house

If you are going to buy a new house, it may be one that has hitherto been simply a private home or one which already provides bed and breakfast. If the latter, and if it has been doing so successfully, do not rush to change its style (or prices): you may forfeit repeat visits from previous guests if you do.

Take the best part of a year, if need be, to house-hunt for what is right for you personally. Conrad Hilton, asked what were the three most important things to consider when setting up a hotel, said 'Location, location, location'; and even in choosing where to run bed and breakfast, not only is the town (or county) vital but the particular street (or village) too. And the neighbours: if these resent an incomer arriving from far afield to trade in their area, or an incursion of visitors' cars (particularly if they park on the road), or the sight of a bed and breakfast notice at your gate, you will not have a very pleasant time. On the other hand, local shops and pubs may well be pleased, and prove very helpful. Staying in the area for a few days (ideally, at the guest-house you are thinking of buying – at its peak period, and at a slack season too), and chatting around, will enable you to get the feel of things. Read the town guidebook and the local paper to obtain background information, call at the nearest Tourist Information Centre, and learn about future plans for the area (a marina to be built? an industrial estate?). The peak buying period is January to April, but you may do better to buy in the autumn and have the winter for redecoration or changes.

Do not be discouraged from buying a badly maintained bed and breakfast house which has therefore been enjoying little trade; provided its price is low, it may be full of potential for improvements and increased custom. Repainting improves a house immediately and at far less cost than, for instance, re-carpeting, so do not be put off if this is all that is needed.

But if it seems good, ask searching questions about why the owner is leaving (fine if he or she is going to retire, expand to a larger place, etc., but not encouraging if lack of guests lies behind the move: ask to see the records of booking for the last three years). Accounts are not very informative, and scrutinising them is a job for an accountant: cynics say some bed and breakfast houses keep three sets – one for themselves, one to impress their bank manager, and one for the income tax inspector. The local Tourist Information Centre may have a good idea how popular this and other such houses in the area are.

Talk to an estate agent and make yourself known – to more than one, if you can, phoning every week or two to find out what's new on his or her books. Read property papers like *Dalton's Weekly* and hotel trade papers which have advertisements for even small bed and breakfast houses (e.g. *Caterer and Hotelkeeper*). And bear in mind that for every £1,000 you pay per lettable bedroom, you will – roughly speaking – need to charge £1 per room per night to justify the expenditure. Sample: £90,000 – including alterations and improvements – for a house with three double rooms = £30 per room (or for doubles, £15 a head). This is a theoretical calculation, of course. The quality of furnishings, and what people are prepared to pay in your area, are major factors likely to affect your charges, whether upwards or downwards.

This is not a book on the basics of how to buy a house (there are plenty of these and a good free one available from branches of the Halifax Building Society) but a few points peculiar to buying a house for bed and breakfast purposes follow.

1 Are there any restrictions in the title deeds or lease on car parking (how much space is there for visitors' cars, and for yours?), on serving drinks (if you want to do this), on displaying signboards, or, indeed, on taking guests for payment? Planning authorities have considerable powers to prevent or permit bed and breakfast enterprises: see below.

2 If fire authority approval is needed (see below), has this been granted? If not, what expenditure will be involved?

3 In a rural area, is there main drainage? If not, will the septic tank be able to cope when there is a houseful of visitors (the Environmental Health Officer can advise)? Similarly, will the present hot water and heating systems be able to cope? Altering drainage systems involves permits and regulations. If you are buying a former farmhouse, you may find you have to pay for water by meter.

4 A building which is in a conservation area, or which has been 'listed' as of architectural or historic interest, is likely to be an attractive one, but there may be problems with even quite minor alterations should you want to make any. If you have the building of an extension in mind, has the present owner ever applied for planning permission for an extension, and been turned down?

5 You will need a fully descriptive inventory of whatever contents you are buying. Are kitchen appliances and cutlery included?

6 Long drives are costly to maintain when used by many visiting cars. Unpruned trees cast gloom in summer: bad for business. Gas may not be laid on; wiring may need redoing.

7 In view of increasing demand for en-suite bathrooms, is there space for these without reducing the number or size of bedrooms available to let? And for the large boiler they will need?

8 Is there storage space for all the extra linen, crockery, etc. you will need (possibly also cots and spare folding beds)?

9 Building societies are not usually interested in bed and
   breakfast houses: can the estate agent tell you of finance
   houses or banks that are?
10 *Where to Live After Retirement* (Consumers' Association) is a
   useful book of do's and don'ts for anyone contemplating a
   move late in life (out of print but perhaps in your public
   library).

Your local library and bookshops will also have books on
house-buying or hotel-buying, such as Miles Quest's *How to buy
your own hotel* (Hutchinson), which is excellent, and the *Step by
Step Guide to Buying a Hotel* (Shoretrade).

Planning permission

If you run a private house for bed and breakfast without having
obtained any necessary planning permission from the local
authority you may, like many, get away with it; but it only
needs a neighbour's complaint (perhaps triggered by your
visitors' cars inconveniently parked because the house has
limited access and parking space) to bring a council inspector
round, followed perhaps by an order telling you to stop taking
paying guests. You may forestall this by asking the planning
authority for written clearance before you begin; it is unlikely to
be withheld if all you are doing is letting a room or two in a
house that is not going to change its character. You might also
fall foul of your insurance company, building society or – in
leasehold or rented property – landlord, if you have not got
their agreement. A useful free booklet is the *Guide to Planning
Permission for Small Businesses* obtainable from the Department of
the Environment (Victoria Road, South Ruislip, Middlesex).
There is no need to accept a planning rejection without
argument. You are entitled to appeal, or to enlist the aid of your
local councillor (even your local MP).

Fire regulations

If more than six people (visitors or staff) sleep in the house, you must have a fire certificate to ensure their safety. The local fire service (address obtainable from town or county hall) will require you to fill in a form, after which your house will be inspected – you may be asked to pay for this. The fire officer will be looking to see whether doors are capable of withstanding fire for a certain period, whether people would readily be able to get out of the house if it were on fire, and perhaps whether fire alarms or fire extinguishers must be put in (also exit signs and emergency lighting). If much expense has to be incurred, you may be able to get a loan under the Fire Precautions (Loans) Act or from the Rural Development Commission; and if you feel excessive requirements are being made, you can appeal and the matter will then go to a magistrates' court (sheriffs' in Scotland).

Sometimes a timber floor or staircase may need fire-resistant board to be added to the underside; doors, or door-frames, may not be fire-resistant, and you may also be required to put self-closing devices on doors: a staircase may have to be enclosed (because flames can sweep up an open stairwell); some wall surfaces may need flame-retardant treatment – not a big problem; and every bedroom may need to have instructions (possibly in several languages) on what to do and where to go if fire breaks out. But no two houses are identical, and it may be that nothing at all needs to be done in your case. Any later alterations that may affect safety should be notified to the fire authority. Fire authorities have the right to enter and inspect any guest-house, and prosecution may follow if it is being operated in contravention of the laws.

To reduce the risk of fire, either ban smoking or provide plenty of big solid ashtrays. For bedrooms, choose fan heaters or other safe appliances (preferably fixed to a wall) rather than radiant ones against which bedclothes may brush; and install plentiful switched sockets at waist level to discourage overloading with adaptors, tugging at flexes, and other hazardous practices. Place a spark-guard around any open fire in the sitting-room when guests go in to dinner. Frying is the commonest cause of kitchen fires; and accumulated boxes and other rubbish can fuel serious fires in attics and cupboards. Some upholstery and flooring materials are very flammable: check before buying, particularly in the case of secondhand chairs. Do not clutter landings with spare beds or cots. See that family and staff understand the need for safe practices.

Fire officers can advise on suitable fire alarms; and on fire extinguishers. Water – best for most fires – is unsuitable, even dangerous, to use on fat or electrical fires. For fats and other flammable liquids, a foam or powder extinguisher is best; for electrical fires, carbon dioxide or powder, never foam. Fire stations have booklets on fire safety, extinguishers and smoke-detector alarms.

Taking over a business

Where the business side of an existing bed and breakfast house is concerned, ask for past years' accounts that your own accountant can scrutinise; enquire what is currently charged for bed and breakfast (and any meals) and how many forward bookings have been made (if deposits have been paid, they should be passed on to you); question the vendor about the sources through which he/she secures visitors and what is spent on publicity (see later chapter). Does he/she employ assistance in the house or garden, will these people continue to work for you if you want them and at what rate of pay (alternatively, should you want to dismiss them, will you have to make redundancy payments)? Has the owner been there long or has there been a succession of owners (a bad sign)? Note that a high level of repeat business in the past will not necessarily continue when you take over, if what generated it was the previous owner's personality or cooking: yours may be better but will take time to get known. If a high proportion of income has been from low-profit meals, rather than from accommodation, this will be bad news.

Be sure you are handed all useful records, such as the visitors' book, when you take over; and that you know where to get access to drains, stopcocks and fuses.

One last point: the name of the house. '249 London Road' does not give a house much identity. And there are so many Old Vicarages and Manor Houses about that they, too, get lost in the crowd. There may be a case for thinking of a new name, with some relevance to the history or situation of the building. Pond Cottage, The Orchard, White Barn, Cliff House, Old Beams, Woody Bank, Riverside or Ivy House all say something which conjures up an attractive image. To avoid misunderstandings, do not call a house '. . . Farm' if there is no longer a farm attached, but use the word 'Farmhouse'. I have found ordinary bed and breakfast houses labelling themselves 'guest-houses', 'hotel' or even 'motel'. Since these terms have varied meanings (in some countries, a 'guest-house' is very downmarket indeed) it is better to avoid such terms altogether rather than mislead people.

4.

Rooms and Gardens

BEDROOMS AND BATHROOMS

Where bedrooms are concerned, and particularly if you want to have no more than six visitors at a time (because of the complications with fire regulations if you take more), you will need to think out carefully the ratio of double or twin rooms, family rooms (capable of taking three or more people) and singles, bearing in mind the likely demand in your area. Minimum sizes are discussed in chapter 8: in a smallish room, twin beds may be better placed against walls and not side by side in the middle of the room. If you buy a pair of twin beds designed for linking together as a double when required, you will have more flexibility (but will need two sets of bedlinen, one set extra-large). Similarly, some bunk beds that can be re-arranged as two singles give you an extra option, if you are prepared for the effort involved.

Washbasins and baths

It is highly advisable to equip each room with a washbasin: and there is an increasing demand for en suite (or at any rate private) bathrooms or showers – with people prepared to pay several pounds more to have these – if rooms are large enough to accommodate them; but remember that every extra bath, toilet or basin means more daily cleaning to be done. If you equip rooms with showers only, there should be a bathroom available elsewhere in the house, as some people are not satisfied with showers; and, if this is also the family bathroom, it should have a cupboard in which the family's washing gear, plastic ducks, pills and so forth can be hidden away.

Equipping the bedrooms

If you want to obtain a listing in your regional Tourist Board's directory of accommodation you will have to put in all the things on the English Tourist Board's list of necessities for approval (see chapter 6). My own recommendations for guests' comfort correspond more to the one crown criteria for bedrooms with additional improvements such as:

Blankets available as an alternative, if preferred, to duvets, and vice versa.

Towels: small for washbasin but four feet or more for shower or bath.

Lighting should include a 60 or 100 watt lamp for reading in bed (two for a double bed), well sited – that is to say, not on a low table so that the lamp is below shoulder-level nor in a non-tiltable shade that prevents light from reaching the book.

Luggage rack, or table suitable to take a suitcase (two in a double room); and shelf for spongebags, etc. (A cheap but neat way to provide racks for suitcases is to keep in each wardrobe a folding melamine picnic-table, as sold by camping shops.)

Clothes storage space may be minimal if you expect only one or two night stays, but anyone coming for a week or more will need adequate drawers and hanging space with at least four good hangers per person (not wire ones); and it does not do for them to find the family's winter woollies in store in their room! Shelves in a built-in wardrobe are easier for room-cleaning provided they give 12 square feet of storage and 3 feet of rail.

Hooks on doors are easy to provide but often lacking. The same is true of hot-water bottles.

Mirrors: your guests may be short or they may be six-footers, so buy long mirrors and site them appropriately, with good lighting.

Television: increasingly, bedrooms rather than sitting-rooms are being equipped with TV so that each person can view the programme of his or her own choice. Occasionally, sets are available only on request, when an aerial extension lead, on a reel, may be useful. At one house I know help-yourself sets are left on the landing. Siting the television on a low table will not do (the screen may be invisible when guests are lying in bed), and if no better position is available the answer may be to install a wall-bracket of the kind specially designed for television sets. Remote control is an extra attraction, worth a mention in your brochure. Reconditioned colour or black-and-white sets, or hire-company surplus ones, are good value; and replacement can be cheaper than repair. Keeping a set in reserve means that no one need be without if a breakdown occurs. (But if your walls are thin, there is a risk that TV or radio will disturb other guests.)

Windows (and heaters) should be childproof.

Locks: In a private house, unlike a hotel, there may be little need for guests to lock their bedrooms when they are out, though a lock on each door is required for 'crown' classification (see chapter 8). Visitors should be able to get into the house whenever they want to, which may mean lending a front-door key. You will need a spare set, since inevitably people go off with keys. A lost front-door key is a security risk: it should not have a house name on it but a Post Office box number.

Sockets (for hair-dryers, shavers, kettles, etc.) are best at waist level for easy access. Shaver sockets need to be variable in design, to accommodate continental shavers.

Tea/coffee: Many good bed and breakfast houses now provide facilities for guests to make tea and coffee whenever they want them, and do not charge extra. Enquiries suggest that people prefer this arrangement to having tea brought up to them on request. A clutter of kettle and cups can be messy (and cause damage to furnishings) but there are many neat wall units which may be preferable (and cost far less than automatic teamaker/alarms, which are another alternative). For instance, Philips make a very compact version for two cups beneath a water-boiling unit. If you do provide a kettle, make sure it is automatic, to avoid condensation. Good quality teabags (or coffee) will be appreciated, as well as sachets of Horlicks, instant hot chocolate etc., and so will fresh milk, although one-portion packs of dried or UHT milk are the norm. I have seen various methods of providing fresh milk: jugs of it handed to visitors when they go to bed, miniature vacuum flasks to keep it cool, large vacuum jugs on the landing. A few houses equip each room with a very small refrigerator for drinks or snacks – not encouraged as a rule – baby food, dog food, diabetics' insulin.

A useful trade supplier of many of the above items is Aliseo – catalogue obtainable from Box D4, Dorking, Surrey.

Hosts often provide a variety of extras without extra charge, and many of these cost them virtually nothing but the effort involved – pot-plants or garden flowers and fruit, the loan of hair-dryer, alarm clock or electric blanket, home-made biscuits, a row of paperbacks. Some put up their own costs, and thus their charges, by providing – in my opinion – far too many 'freebies' such as chocolates, bottles of mineral water, newspapers, sewing-kits, scent and hand cream, shampoo and bath essence, even toothpaste and first-aid kits. Probably these things are provided in an attempt to emulate the hotel chains, which is a pretentious aim for a modest bed and breakfast house. It is much better for bed and breakfast houses to provide services that the average big hotel cannot: use of washing and ironing facilities (sometimes for a small charge) is an example, particularly valuable to overseas visitors doing a prolonged tour of Britain; or of car-washing gear. A box of shoe polish and brushes on the landing is helpful. Really good armchairs (if there is space) are an asset, particularly if your sitting-room is not very large or if the view from the bedroom is worth enjoying. If you are going to do all the cleaning yourself, everything should be chosen for ease of maintenance. A carefully thought-out room (e.g. fitted wool carpet) should take no more than 15 – 20 minutes to do each day.

Three money-saving tips: there are several mail-order suppliers of very inexpensive chipboard tables which can look attractive if covered with a floor-length cloth, see Appendix. For built-in cupboards and bath sides, Far Eastern plywood in eight by four foot sheets to varnish before being cut to size looks almost as good as solid mahogany. Parker Knoll fireside-style armchairs are solid enough to be worth buying secondhand for re-upholstering.

Beds and bedding

And what about the beds – the most vital element in bed and breakfast and sometimes the most neglected? Every owner should sleep on each mattress at least once a year and consider what it would feel like to a heavy guest or one with a bad back. Another test is to place one arm under and one arm over the mattress, then press the two together. If one hand can detect the pressure of the other, the mattress if due for renewal.

Like carpets, beds are costly to buy, but buying cheap ones is a false economy as a mattress will soon need renewal. If you spend a reasonable sum (at the time of writing, the best part of £100 for a single mattress) you may expect many years' life from it. You will not get repeat visits, or recommendations, from visitors who have had a miserable night's sleep on an inferior mattress. As one wrote to me: 'I cut short my stay because I could not have slept one more night riding that roller-coaster!' Bear in mind that extra-firm beds are more popular than soft ones, firm edges are desirable because guests often sit on beds, and – for your own sake when cleaning the room – smooth-running castors are important. Bases with solid tops last longer than sprung ones. Underbed drawers make useful linen stores, if you don't need to move the bed.

The choice of bedding is almost as critical. Waterproof covers (plus underblankets) for children's mattresses were discussed in chapter 1. An alternative is a very thick cotton underblanket, or else the Cumulus mattress protector (polyester filled) which fits smoothly over corners, without need for tying, is moisture-resistant and can be washed. Fitted undersheets make bedmaking easier; so do duvets, except for one-night visitors, but not all guests like these, finding them sometimes too hot and bulky. Duvets vary in thickness and warmth from 4 to 13 tog rating; some come in two separate layers to give a choice. Slipping covers on and off is easier if you can make your own covers with press-studs or Velcro down one side as well as along the bottom: surprisingly, I do not know of any manufactured like this. Washable paper undercovers help to keep pillows in good condition. Duvets and pillows that are machine-washable and quick-drying (e.g. polyester fibre fillings) may prove to be a useful choice, bearing in mind that occasionally you may get a visitor (or visitor's dog) who soils them, and washable bed-spreads too are best – suitcases, dogs and feet still in shoes are bound to dirty them. Although some people may be happy with one pillow, have a second ready in each wardrobe for those who need it (and an extra blanket). And regularly replace pillows that have become skinny (or take them to a cleaner for recon-ditioning): they need cost very little these days. The test is to place one across your extended arm, and if it droops down it is time to get rid of it.

Changing, laundering and ironing bedlinen is one of the biggest chores (slightly reduced if you have washing-machine and tumble-dryer upstairs, not down; and if you put linen in folded not rumpled), particularly if you have many one-night guests. People staying longer certainly appreciate it if linen is changed more than once a week, and hand-towels daily – though for the latter the most important requirement is dryness, which may be achieved by having a heated towel-rail. It is not use but frequent laundering which wears out towels etc., and your stock of such things will need to be big unless you keep to quick-drying fabrics where appropriate. Having all linen the same colour makes things simpler, too. There are linen-hire services which do all the laundering, but this may not be an economical service for small houses: enquire locally.

At some houses which take residents in winter for long stays at low rates, the best bedspreads, etc. are removed and cheap ones substituted for that period, with the whole room redecor-ated in spring in light fresh colours to maintain good standards for the ordinary visitors of summer.

Four-posters (rarely genuine) are in vogue now, and often more is charged for a bedroom with one. Attractive alterna-tives, in some ways more practical, are half-testers or wall-mounted canopies. Ernest Thompson (who himself runs a bed and breakfast house in Sussex) has invented and sells a kit for converting an existing bed into a four-poster. But, like large Victorian wardrobes, over-big beds can make a room seem cramped.

Finally, be sure to provide instructions – written or oral – for operating the controls of heaters, TV, radio alarms and showers, and information about meal times.

Bathrooms

It is now possible to put in additional lavatories (en suite or otherwise) with a minimum of trouble or expense and very little structural alteration. No longer is a four-inch wastepipe needed: a three-quarter-inch one suffices, so neat that it can even run along skirtings or over door-frames if need be. It is connected to the w.c. pan via an electrically operated unit which, when the w.c. is flushed, liquidises all waste material and pumps it away through the pipe in about a quarter of a minute. Such a lavatory can go under the stairs, or be built-in on a landing or in a bedroom – with, of course, an extractor fan for ventilation where there is no window.

It goes without saying that scrupulous cleaning at least once a day is going to be needed. (Anxieties about catching AIDS are, in this context, exaggerated, but wearing disposable plastic-film gloves may be a reassurance.) A spare toilet-roll should always be on view and a sanibin provided, as even so-called disposable products can clog drains and septic tanks.

It is not a good idea to make guests rely on a lavatory in a bathroom if there is no other available. It only needs one person to settle down to a long soak for an unhappy queue to build up outside. (This problem is a common cause of dissatisfaction.)

Showers take up little space and use far less hot water than baths, but not every guest likes them and they vary greatly in efficiency and general comfort – particularly those which are merely plastic cabinets with their own instantaneous electric water-heater inside. Whichever you choose, the cabinet will need almost as much cleaning as a bath and, except in a soft-water area, the shower nozzle will have to be regularly descaled. Disposable shower caps should be provided. Check before buying whether your water pressure will give an adequate flow for the task; whether the controls will be easily understood and manipulated by someone unfamiliar with them; and whether the cabinet is roomy enough for a large person. Make adequate provision for carrying away the steam, or condensation will harm walls and ceilings.

When choosing a new bath, once again remember the possible size of your guests, and do not be tempted to buy a short or narrow bath simply because space is at a premium. (A small washbasin, possibly, but a six-foot bath, though the larger the bath the more hot water needed.) Oval ones, for corners, may look pretty but are usually much too short. Grab rails for elderly users are desirable to prevent falls, as well as a non-slip surface on the bottom of the bath. If there is a shower attached to the bath taps, its position on the wall should be adjustable to various heights. A neat alternative to a shower curtain, which may look tacky and can lead to trouble if carelessly left hanging outside the bath, is a hinged glass screen; or else a roller-blind designed for the purpose. A pop-up bath plug is preferable to one on a chain which will inevitably get tugged off one day.

If you do not want the expense, and waste, of providing a fresh miniature tablet of good quality soap for each visitor (particularly one-nighters), an alternative is to buy a good liquid soap in a dispenser, preferable to supplying cheap soap, or one cake only to be used by a succession of visitors.

The greatest essential is that the hot water supply should be reliable, adequate for successive baths, hot enough for shaving, and able to supply peak demands in the morning and evening: more on water heating in chapter 5. And, if you do contemplate spending thousands on creating an en suite bathroom, be really sure there will be enough guests willing to pay several pounds a night more for this, to justify the expense (and, sometimes, the loss of other bedrooms to make space).

Although a guest room may not get such constant use as your own bedroom, it needs to be kept immaculate, and emulsion paint is the easiest thing to renew frequently. If you employ a decorator, a guarantee of completion on time is more important than a low price, for a room out of action is income lost. Otherwise, choose washable wallpapers; and also use carpets that are neither shaggy nor pale. In a bathroom, a sheet material will be better than tiles, and a light colour shows up marks less than a dark one.

THE SITTING-ROOM

Particularly if evening meals are served, an attractive and comfortable place in which to sit afterwards is essential (preferably not combined with the dining-room), and it is mostly here that contact is made between host and guest, or guest and guest: one of the principal satisfactions of running a successful bed and breakfast house. Even if you provide only bed and breakfast, a guests' sitting-room is an asset, especially if you are one of those hosts or hostesses (the majority?) who offer tea or coffee and biscuits or cake at the end of the evening. Whatever you provide can legitimately be reflected in the prices you charge.

Decoration

It is worth giving careful thought to the kind of background you are going to create in the sitting-room. Matters of pure taste apart, the commonest decorating mistake is failure to appreciate scale: large-patterned curtains in cottagey rooms, furniture designed for compact modern houses looking lost in spacious old ones; high ceilinged Victorian rooms papered with tiny floral designs. An ill-judged assortment of clashing fabric patterns and miscellaneous saleroom furniture, dowdy wallpaper and dim lighting (here or elsewhere) is not going to bring visitors back a second time. Nor should family clutter intrude. If in doubt about a plan of decoration, you can get expert help inexpensively from the interior design services of magazines like *Good Housekeeping*, from paint and wallpaper firms or department stores, and from the books of co-ordinated schemes published by, for instance, Laura Ashley or Habitat. *Which?* (February 1987) found such services a reliable source of ideas and also briefly reviewed a number of books on interior design.

Make the most of whatever features the room has, whether a marble fireplace that needs restoring, decorative plasterwork on the ceiling to pick out in colour, or handsome brass door fittings that deserve to be well polished.

Furnishing

Armchairs, which should be ample in size and firmly upholstered, are an expensive item – and there need to be enough for the maximum number of guests you expect. Buying second-hand chairs in poor shape, or turning a blind eye to the age and decrepit springs of what you already have, is unwise if you care for your visitors' comfort. Since visitors come in all shapes and sizes, a lot of identical chairs only ensure that some guests are uncomfortable, and they look institutional too. Nor is a standard three-piece suite a good idea, though an assortment of chairs should have some uniformity of style or covering. An upright armchair is usually preferred by an older person. Several bed and breakfast owners daunted by the high cost of getting chairs re-upholstered have – after going to WI or evening classes, or studying do-it-yourself books – set to and learnt how to do the job themselves during the winter lull. Soft background lighting needs to be supplemented by standard or table lamps that give a good light for reading. Unlike those in bedrooms, carpets in sitting-rooms (and on stairs) will get more than average use and so should be not only of durable quality but cleanable too: I know of nothing better than an 80% wool mixture.

Entertainments and displays

There are arguments for and against providing television here (or record players, piano etc.) since this kills conversation; but a supply of books, magazines, the local paper, cards and board games will add to visitors' pleasure at little extra cost to yourself. Pictures of local views or by local artists, flowers or pot-plants, local crafts, antiques or curios, things you have made (patchwork cushions, dried flower arrangements) or which you collect (clocks, snuff-boxes), all help to give a room character and will interest visitors. Articles for sale will add to your profits, and many a bed and breakfast house sells antiques, paintings or crafts as a sideline. And as a focal point there is nothing more attractive than a crackling fire – and not only in winter – particularly for visitors whose own homes have only central heating.

Additional rooms

If it is possible, it is a very good idea to have a second room available, to which TV or smokers can be confined; or a games-room for things like snooker, table-tennis and darts. A few owners have even set up, for their own use too, rooms with exercise equipment, sunbed, Jacuzzi, sauna, etc. – like everything else a tax-deductible expense if it is one of the services installed for visitors, who may be willing to pay extra for the use of such things. A conservatory may provide the extra room needed; consider also the potential of cellar or attic conversions. It is no good providing numerous bedrooms if the provision of sitting-room (or equivalent) space is not in proportion. In some houses, taking down a wall in order to combine hall and sitting-room is the answer (provided there is a porch or lobby at the front door).

The more you provide, the greater will be the number of repeat visits and recommendations. If you are in an area where there is much competition, it is important to offer just that little bit more or better than rival bed and breakfast houses.

The extent to which you join your guests in the sitting-room depends on your preferences and theirs, which will vary. Some will want to come and go as they please (and may welcome a separate entrance) without making much contact with you; others, especially English-speakers from abroad, will regard conversation with their host and hostess as one of the pleasures of the holiday. I know places where guests have felt shunned by their hosts, others where they have left early because they seemed to have no time to themselves! Only your own tact and discretion can guide you.

Conferences

If you have a room capable of seating ten or more people, a useful supplement to your bed and breakfast income might be accommodating small business seminars and meetings during the daytime, particularly if you or an outside caterer can provide a buffet lunch and drinks too; or providing tea for a minibus of old people on a day's outing. But the room needs to be immaculate and businesslike; and adequate car parking will be needed. Much depends on whether you are near a business centre or motorway. A letter saying what you can offer should be sent to firms within a small radius (say, a half-hour drive), the names of which can be gathered from the Yellow Pages and Thomson local directories or by asking the local Chamber of Commerce or Rotary Club for advice. The English Tourist Board has a booklet on *The Mini-Conference Market*. Business firms pay well, and their needs continue outside the peak periods for tourism.

THE KITCHEN

Even if you have not been accustomed to catering for more than a family, the skill of cooking for somewhat larger numbers is not difficult to acquire. If you are unaccustomed to cooking for numbers, try out intended menus beforehand on parties of friends by way of dress-rehearsals. But, first things first: can your kitchen cope, particularly if you are going to offer evening meals as well as breakfasts?

You will need storage space for the extra china, glass and cutlery to be bought, as well as room for sufficient chairs and tables – say 16 square feet per person (how many beds you have should determine the size of the dining-room). In some houses, everybody eats at one big table: do you intend to seat guests together or separately? To eat with them or leave them alone?

You may need to buy large saucepans and other equipment, such as a big food-processor. Are your refrigerator and freezer big enough? Your cooker? Your food cupboards? Your dish-washer? It may be that replanning your kitchen should take priority over many other projects, in which case bear in mind that many items (toasters, scales, etc.) can be wall-mounted to save space. This may be an opportunity, if you are shorter or taller than average, to have worktops positioned lower or higher than is standard practice: you are going to spend more time in the kitchen, and wrong heights cause backache.

A few hosts encourage their guests to enter their kitchens, and even to use them for making tea, etc., and some use them to demonstrate recipes as a sideline, which brings in some useful business at slack periods: bear these possibilities in mind when replanning, as the kitchen will have to be thoroughly present-able for such uses. There may also be things you will want to do in the future which you have not contemplated before, like adding to your range an ice cream and sorbet maker or a yogurt maker, an electric deep-fryer or a rice-cooker.

Planning the kitchen

If you have the chance to plan a kitchen from scratch, try to arrange it to minimise walking. A good work sequence is to have storage for vegetables, etc. adjacent to sink and waste-disposal, with a very large dishwasher next, followed by china storage. A large worktop next to the cooker is important: with similar space near the dining-room door (for dishes waiting to be taken in) perhaps with a hot tray to keep plates warm. Some-times changing the position of the door into the dining-room can make life a lot easier. Allow space for equipment which, even if you do not have now, you may want in the future – such things as a large urn for boiling water (to speed up tea, coffee, eggs, etc.); a scullery with extra-big washing-machine, tumble-dryer and rotary ironer; refrigerator space may be needed for chilling drinks, whether provided by you or brought in by visitors; a big freezer.

A microwave cooker does far more than defrost or heat up: it is particularly good for the swift cooking of fish, vegetables, scrambled eggs, bacon and tomatoes, sauces, jacket potatoes, baked apples, stuffed mushrooms, and much else. If you want to offer snack meals at any hour, a sandwich-toaster is a useful accessory. A six-pint slow cooker is ideal for trouble-free braising – even pheasants or pigeons, for instance – providing main courses that will not spoil if guests are late. Electric slicers and knives are real labour-savers when there is much cutting up to be done. An electric fruit-squeezer helps you to offer that rare pleasure – fresh orange-juice at breakfast. You can have your own coffee-roaster and grinder; electric vegetable peelers; sauce makers; woks for stir-fries; waffle makers (to keep Americans happy!); and (for those who 'can't boil an egg') an automatic egg boiler. To keep cooking-smells out of the dining-room, a powerful air-extractor is a good idea. Use the dishwasher to clean more than dishes (e.g. trays, bathroom beakers, chandelier drops, ashtrays, even brushes if they will stand a high temperature).

Crockery

The choice of crockery is important, as you will need a lot of it. Questions to ask are: will the pattern be replaceable (avoid foreign makes)? Are the pieces stable, and designed to stack? Is the china break-resistant? (This usually means buying catering quality; except, perhaps, for cups because these tend to be unpleasantly thick – sometimes the same pattern is available in both catering and ordinary quality.) Is it a reasonable weight (a trayful should not be too heavy to carry easily)? Is it dishwasher-proof? Microwave-proof? Dual-purpose pieces save expense and space; examples are soup/cereal bowls and tea/side plates. You will need only small toastracks (in large ones, toast goes cold before all is eaten) but teapots in two sizes (one pint for two people, one and a half pints for four) and coffeepots likewise (half-pint and one pint, with half-pint jugs for hot milk).

THE GROUNDS

Any garden is a potential asset, unless neglected. Visitors appreciate even a small patio, verandah or even roof terrace on a town house where, surrounded by flower tubs, they may sit or sunbathe. Some hosts offer to bring drinks or breakfast outdoors on fine days.

Using your grounds

Consider the following list of uses to which some gardens lend themselves:

croquet, swingball, putting, tennis, badminton;
a children's play area with sandpit, swing, etc. (separate from the rest of the garden);
swimming pool;
barbecue;
growing vegetables, fruit or herbs;
beekeeping;
chickens for free-range eggs;
greenhouse to raise pot-plants for the house, tomatoes, early salads;
bird-table or birdbath within view of the breakfast room.

If you have many acres, particularly of woodland, it may lend itself to marking out a nature trail. (At a Sussex farm, month-by-month field notes are given to visitors, with a map, telling them what wildlife and crops they can see.)

A garden is hard work to keep in order and, when busy with visitors, you will have limited time to spend on it, so it may be worth investing in the biggest possible lawnmower and in shrubs, groundcover plants and other perennials that keep weeds at bay and need little attention. A large lawn, though it may be attractive, needs frequent mowing in the summer. The labour could be reduced by laying paving or cobbles instead (but not concrete or tarmac!) which would also provide a hard-wearing sitting area if equipped with garden furniture.

The front garden

The front garden is what gives visitors the first impression of the house, so it is essential that it should look good. Sometimes approaches to houses are ruined by the siting of car parks right in front; by glimpses of dustbins, crates and other mess; by clothes-lines or washing visible; and by the appearance of the house exterior itself – neglected paintwork, windows that need cleaning, dingy curtains, and the door plastered with plaques or labels (AA, Tourist Board, credit cards and so forth) which, far from being impressive give a very downmarket look to any house, particularly when there is a plethora of them.

So keep bins, etc. out of sight, if necessary by putting up a simple screen of larch-lap panels, board fencing, or a trellis with a climbing plant over it. And encourage car parking away from the house (though allowing temporary access to the front door with suitcases).

Your signboard

You will need a sign at the gate. This need be no more than the name of the house if all your visitors are booked in advance, but make sure that it is easily legible from a moving car (no fancy patterns or 'ye olde' lettering that cannot be quickly made out by a driver), and check that it is visible from a distance in either direction, so that drivers do not go past it and then have to reverse. If you are open for passing trade, the sign will have to be large enough to announce the fact (a sign under 1.2 square metres does not usually need planning permission), and to say if you offer evening meals. If your house is not visible from the road, your sign is particularly important, and with a long frontage a sign at each end may be advisable. Larger signs, and more than one sign on the same road, will need planning permission. Whether or not you will get it, with or without conditions, depends on the policy of the planning authority (which may be particularly stringent in a national park). Your planning authority will give you informal advice and send you a copy of an explanatory government booklet. A sign must be well made of durable materials. If painted, it should be done by a professional signwriter and have a weatherproof finish. Nothing is less inviting than a tottering sign with amateurish lettering and peeling paint.

Water

Water is always an asset. I have seen a pool previously inaccessible to visitors (behind a hedge) opened up by a pathway, with a paved area alongside where tea is now taken while visitors watch the ducks.

If there is a river or lake, consider its potential for boating, fishing, swimming or, in winter, skating (provided it is safely shallow). An area of low ground can be deliberately flooded when the weather reaches freezing-point, and skates are lent to visitors.

As to swimming pools, it has been found that they get very little use if their temperature is under 30°C, and even then not much if the air is chilly. A swimming pool may reach this temperature on a hot day even if unheated, particularly if it has been prevented from cooling much overnight: a sheet of plastic 'bubble' material pulled over the water's surface does the trick and keeps leaves out. Alternatively, an outdoor pool can be enclosed – not necessarily a very expensive business if you use an inflatable dome with a fan to keep air constantly filling the vinyl cover. Such a cover reduces any water-heating costs by nearly half, and reduces the task of cleaning too. A floodlight prolongs the use of a pool on summer evenings.

There are also ways of achieving an indoor pool, usable all the year round, at less cost than you might suppose: for instance, by putting it in a superfluous stable or barn. This will obviously limit its size, but there will be plenty of room for at least an exercise pool (say eight feet by six) with a Jetstream to provide water-massage: good therapy for weary walkers or anglers, among others! To put up a separate building or extension for a swimming pool is not only costly but involves planning permission. One expedient is to choose a log cabin design for the purpose. A covered pool can be locked up to ensure children's safety.

It is important to have the installation done by an expert in the problems involved (such as condensation and heat-conservation): a list of reputable installers can be obtained from the Swimming Pool Association, 1a Junction Road, Andover, Hants, whose members are pledged to provide after-sales service and insurance. A later chapter deals with grants and loans available to help with the costs involved, and possible tax concessions. For safety, make it a rule that no guest uses the pool alone, and make sure your public liability insurance covers you against accidents in the pool. (A useful book, *Take the Plunge*, is obtainable for £7.50 from the English Tourist Board, 4 Bromells Road, London SW4 0BJ.)

Money spent on garden amenities not only may add to the value of your property, and to your own pleasure in it, but may be eligible for loans or grants in the same way as building improvements (see later chapter); while garden (like house) maintenance will qualify for tax relief as a business expenditure.

Outdoor lighting

An attractive garden – even one particularly attractive tree – may be worth spotlighting at night. Outdoor lighting can enable visitors to go on enjoying their after-dinner coffee and conversation in the open air; and (if you want this) may attract the attention of passers-by who could be possible future customers. It should be expertly installed for safety.

Garden produce

If you are a gardener, you will know enough about your own and your garden's capabilities for food production. While bulky and low-value vegetables such as root crops may not be economic in terms of space and work, some things are worth growing because they will be fresher (lettuce, for example) or much cheaper (some legumes) than shop-bought ones, or because, like many herbs, they are otherwise unobtainable. Most soft fruit requires little attention during the summer except for picking (and some visitors may do this for you!); it is invaluable for jam and to freeze for pies and puddings. Fruit trees take time to come into production, but they can be decorative in themselves, especially if grown in cordon or espalier form.

Record any expenditure on the garden, including casual labour, for your accountant to claim as a tax-deductible business expense.

If you garden organically (which means using no artificial fertilisers or pesticides at all) and serve only your own or other organically grown produce, you will be able to publicise this fact as an attraction to the growing number of people to whom an organic diet is important.

5.
Catering

BREAKFAST

Many people like making their own assortment from a choice of starters at breakfast-time – particularly if you provide plenty of options: several cereals, fruit (fresh or stewed), juices, yogurt, muesli (perhaps home-made). You may find that guests then eat less of the main course. (One thing *not* to offer on a self-service basis is – a disagreeable feature of some chain hotels – fried eggs drying up on a hot-tray.)

However, most bed and breakfast hosts say their visitors – unless they are on a diet – almost invariably do opt for a 'full British breakfast' to follow: eggs, bacon, and as many extras as your budget allows – mushrooms, tomatoes, sausages, fried bread, kidneys, black pudding or baked beans. Because some visitors who have been touring for a fortnight may by now be bored with this, it is a good idea to have some alternatives available such as omelettes, smoked haddock, kedgeree, kippers, ham or tongue, mackerel, porridge and cream (with whisky!), fishcakes, Arbroath smokies from Scotland, potato cakes with bacon, croissants or muffins (it is possible to buy toasters wide enough to take these), waffles or pancakes with maple syrup (American-style), devilled mushrooms ... there are plenty of alternatives. (A guest-house in Cumbria got featured on television because a breakfast list running to 200 items was on offer.)

It will be a real treat for your visitors if you can offer free-range eggs, home-baked bread, and your own jams and marmalade or honey. The deep impression created on visitors by homemade bread and hot breakfast rolls (including *good* whole-meal if you can master it) is quite out of proportion to the little extra work involved – and it is an economy at that! As with any other home produce – eggs, milk, cream, fruit – you can afford to be generous for the sake of a good impression, as there is a limit to how much anyone can eat of them. If you yourself have no time for making preserves or bread, a local person may be willing (the Women's Institute might put you in touch with someone). Full marks if your orange-juice is freshly squeezed and if you can offer a choice of teas, as well as really top-quality coffee, never instant. Most people prefer hot milk with coffee. Keeping coffee-maker and toaster in the breakfast room, and encouraging guests to help themselves, takes a little of the action out of the busy kitchen.

There are arguments for and against one-portion packs of butter (or sunflower margarine). For: hygiene, and less waste. Against: a very much higher cost per pound, fiddly for visitors to open, and a cafeteria image. It is not difficult to slice a half-pound pack of butter into small pats and put them on ice. I can think of nothing in favour of one-portion packs of marmalade when compared with a generous pot of good-quality preserve.

Some hosts require all their visitors to take breakfast at a fixed time. Others are more flexible (it is easier to cook each breakfast if visitors do not all come down at once), asking guests the previous night when it is wanted and sometimes also what they want to eat.

It is a good idea to do some breakfast preparation the night before, particularly if you have to cater for early-risers catching planes or with business appointments; laying tables, setting out cereals and preserves, putting teapots and plates ready to warm, preparing porridge, taking eggs from the refrigerator (and putting into it jugs of fruit juice or bowls of fruit), defrosting freezer supplies. Frozen supplies (bacon, sausages, bread, butter, yogurt) are very useful when the numbers to be catered for are unpredictable – so are other emergency supplies such as mushrooms, tomatoes and grapefruit, and cartons of longlife milk.

It costs nothing to lay out your own morning newspaper for guests to read.

53

At a few houses, there is a choice of 'continental' or 'British' breakfast, with a difference in price, for people who do not want a big cooked meal.

Where breakfast in bed is an option it may be continental only, and sometimes (as with early morning tea brought up on a tray) a small charge is made for this service – which is not greatly in demand, however. Small extra services like this can be entrusted to the children if they are of the right age, and they will be glad of the tips they may get.

LUNCH

It is not usual for a bed and breakfast house to offer lunch, but many will fill vacuum flasks or even provide packed lunches. Some (particularly if no cooked meal is offered in the evening) are prepared to make snacks like toasted sandwiches or a 'ploughman's'.

DINNER

Dinners vary tremendously, from shepherd's pie and stewed fruit at 6.30 p.m. to a four-course cordon bleu meal at 7.30 or 8 p.m. with silver, crystal and candles on the table. The occasional barbecue is popular, too. Arguments for a particular time (which should be stated on your brochure) are balanced – here are some for an early evening meal:

some people are used to it;
it suits younger children;
it leaves a longer evening for entertainment, or the pub, or a stroll;
walkers, etc. get hungry early at the end of a hard day;
from your own point of view, clearing away and washing up do not drag on until late in the evening, and casual kitchen help (older schoolchildren?) is not available later.

Arguments for a late meal include:

other people are used to it, and it is a more appropriate time for
    more elaborate meals;
visitors do not have to curtail their day's outing;
parents of very young children can put them to bed first.

Not many hosts actually ask their visitors' preference, however. To some extent, the time of the meal, the style of the food,
and the visitors you will get all affect each other.

Menus

Whether a choice of dishes is offered at each course of a fixed-
price meal varies from house to house: those who are coping
single-handed, or who want to avoid waste in order to keep their
charges down, do not offer choices, but they must be prepared
to have some alternative in reserve if it turns out that a visitor
is, for instance, a vegetarian or hates fish or whatever. Some
offer two fixed menus: a simple and inexpensive one, and a
cordon bleu one costing half as much again. Another compromise is to offer a choice of starters and puddings (which is
not difficult, as many of these can be prepared in advance and
leftovers can often be frozen), but not of the main course.
Avoiding long pauses between courses, never popular with
hungry diners, is easier if your menu is simple.

If you are an adventurous cook, it may nevertheless be wise
to offer a relatively plain dish on the first day of a visit, until you
have ascertained whether or not your guest is happy with garlic,
game or whatever else is in your repertoire (the average Briton's
favourite meal is prawn cocktail, steak, and a gâteau). A very
popular policy is to use as much local produce and as many
home-grown vegetables and local recipes as you can, if your
house is in an area which lends itself to this. There are several
directories to help you find local specialities (e.g. *British Food
Finds* published by Rich & Green, and *Good Food Directory,*
Consumers' Association). Do not have a fixed rota of dishes
which disregards what produce is best at the time; and, above
all, learn from leftovers on plates what is unpopular. Do not

repeat the same menu in a fortnight. Keep a note of guests' preferences if you are hoping for repeat bookings.

One of the principal ways in which the modest bed and breakfast house is, or can be, superior to nearly every hotel is home cooking: food freshly prepared for the visitors, using none of the convenience foods beloved of the catering industry, and concentrating on the best of British dishes rather than pale imitations of international cuisine. Overseas visitors love this, and so do many of the natives for whom Lancashire hotpot or treacle tart are a half-forgotten memory. Serve apple cake in Dorset, rum nicky in Cumberland, or really good pasties in Cornwall and you will find visitors asking for the recipes to take home.

Although saving yourself unnecessary work, and doing as much preparation ahead as possible, it is undesirable to copy such tricks of professional caterers as using powder soups, boil-in-the-bag dishes, precooked meat cooled for slicing and then reheated later, precooked vegetables reheated by microwave, and so on. Making your own casseroles, pâtés, fruit pies, soups, etc. and freezing them is good practice because quality does not suffer and yet you always have something that can be produced quickly for unexpected guests. There will sometimes be a guest who does not like what is on your menu for the day, and it is useful to have some alternatives available behind the scenes – including a vegetarian option.

In some houses, there is an à la carte list available in addition to the fixed menu, with each dish separately and rather highly priced to reflect the extra trouble involved. A compromise method is to offer several options but ask visitors to make their choice after breakfast, to save wasted ingredients and effort.

To serve or not to serve?

Some people say they will not do dinners because they cannot make a profit on them, there are good cheap meals to be had at nearby pubs or restaurants, or the work is too much. Others say this is where much of their profit comes from, there is nowhere else to eat within walking distance, and much of their own enjoyment comes from cooking for (and talking to) their visitors. There are no fixed rules, except that visitors tend to book for shorter stays at places which do not provide evening meals. Some visitors like dining around at a different place each night (if you want to discourage this, let them see your dinner menu before they leave the breakfast table). Those who have had a strenuous day usually prefer to stay in if they can, as do many elderly people and families with young children.

The most important thing if you provide dinner is to keep up a consistent standard, not aiming so high that from time to time you have a flop which will make an indelible dent in your reputation. Your child may fall ill or the plumbing seize up, but guests will still have to be fed, so plan menus that can be to some extent prepared in advance; then, whatever the emergency, you will be under less stress.

There are a few bed and breakfast houses – possibly the spearhead of a growing trend? – which offer an element of self-catering. Though breakfast (only) is served by the proprietor, a kitchen for guests' use is available – not fully equipped but suitable for making snack suppers, heating readymade or take-away dishes, and so on. This greatly appeals to the type of family which takes its main meal out in the middle of the day; or wants flexible times for eating in the evening (determined by children's bed-times, TV viewing or whatever); or which needs to economise. At a few such houses, owners make a useful profit by stocking a freezer with home-made dishes for sale – such as fish pies, macaroni cheese, shepherd's pie, flans, or ready-cooked chickens. Since such cooking in bulk is little harder than cooking one-off meals, and can be done at any convenient season, this is an idea well worth considering. In fact, merely providing a small microwave oven may be all that is needed.

At a few houses, dinners are in fact prepared not by the owner but by a friend who comes in: he or she takes whatever the visitors pay, less a percentage to the owner. And there are others where dinner is available only on certain evenings in the week, sometimes with an arrangement at a local restaurant to feed guests on the other nights, often for a discounted price if those nights are ones when the restaurant's trade is slack.

Serving dinners, buffet meals or Sunday lunches to nonresident locals can be a profitable sideline in slack periods, as can outside catering on a minor scale.

SNACKS

It is easy to make a few scones or biscuits (greatly preferable to most packet stuff) to put on a welcoming tray of tea for new arrivals (something which most good bed and breakfast houses invariably offer, usually without charge), or of hot drinks before bedtime – almost a necessity at farms or other houses where the evening meal is served very early. At some houses, cream teas are served to passers-by, some of whom are then suitably impressed and decide to stay.

DRINKS

There is no reason why soft drinks should not be sold to guests (apple or grape juice, alcohol-free lager, cola, etc.), but wines and spirits are in a different category. A Gallup poll found four out of five people like to have wine with their dinner, but for this a residential licence is needed; and to get one you have to apply to the local court, where justices decide applications at sessions held six times a year. Your solicitor can help you do this – his or her fee costs more than the licence. The local authority has to be notified (the licence may affect your rateable value), and an announcement put in the local paper. You may find that your nearest pub raises objections, or that the fire authorities want to inspect your premises and propose changes. The police will check on your probity. Some people find the difficulties too much to make the licence worth having; others find everything goes through without a hitch. It all seems to depend on where you live. You can, however, make a good deal of profit by putting up to 25% on wine (30% on spirits) bought at (for instance) your local cash and carry.

There is no objection to visitors bringing in their own wine or other drinks, nor to your giving them a glass, as you might a friend. But you could be in trouble if you bill them for drink you have supplied if you have no licence. A residential licence means you can serve drinks at any hour, but only to guests (and their friends). A table licence entitles you to serve non-residents dining at the house. You have to reapply annually. If you have a drinks licence, it is vital not to be late in renewing it. One owner sent in her renewal a mere 48 hours too late (she had been on holiday). The court cancelled the licence she had held for 20 years, and insisted she apply for a new one. This cost her £200 in solicitor's fees; £200 to an architect because, following re-inspection, a structural change was demanded; £2000 for the change itself. And meantime, loss of trade.

You are usually expected to have a separate sitting-room and sufficient toilets; and to sell soft drinks too. You must sell drinks in official measures and display their prices. You may not serve alcohol to under-18s. Ask the licensing inspector of the local police for advice. Drinks licences are issued to individuals and do not go with the premises; you cannot automatically take over the licence of the previous owner of a house. When buying a property with one, check that the house plans held at the licensing court still truly represent what you are now taking over: otherwise, you might not get your licence.

The other things to consider (about serving pre-dinner drinks in particular) are the money (including duty and tax) tied up in the stock, where you will keep it, who will serve it (at an hour when you are likely to be busy in the kitchen), and security from pilferage or burglary. Provided you have the right kind of clientele, you could follow the example of many houses where visitors help themselves from a tray of drinks (with a measure) or from miniatures, and write down what they have had. Provide a list of what you charge per drink.

As to buying table wines, there was a very warm recommendation of the Majestic Wine Warehouses chain for value and choice in *Caterer and Hotelkeeper* magazine. They operate on a cash and carry, delivery or mail order basis. You could take a local basic course in choosing wine.

Coffee and tea

Serving unlimited help-yourself coffee in the sitting-room is not only generous but frees the dining-room for you to clear up. Providing mints is popular but not very imaginative: alternatives include petits fours, real Turkish delight, florentines or fudge – preferably home-made – or a local speciality such as Kendal mint cake.

BACKGROUND MUSIC

Do you want to provide background music in the dining-room? A tricky matter! For one thing, although it breaks the silence in a room where at first no one is talking, some of your visitors will actively dislike it (pop? Mantovani? Schubert? – you will not please everyone) unless you keep the volume well down. Secondly, you may inadvertently break the law. One restaurateur who played records for his customers' enjoyment suddenly got a £340 bill from the Performing Rights Society for reproducing recorded music in public (every performer is entitled to a fee when this happens to his or her music). Showing TV or video films to the public is another potentially dodgy area.

COSTING MEALS

It is essential to know whether you are making a profit or loss on meals, particularly dinners. It is not difficult to work out what the food for breakfast costs – probably around 70p – £1 a head, for what each guest eats differs little – but dinners are far more variable (and with a greater likelihood of food wasted, too, particularly if several choices are offered). To food costs has to be added something in respect of fuel, renewals of tableware and all the overheads of the house – and the labour involved.

This is one reason why it can be useful to attend one of the catering courses referred to in chapter 10, because although you may know how to cook, you may not know how to determine the cost per meal and therefore what you should be charging.

Some people think out a dozen menus which they serve in rotation (and so, subject to price fluctuations, can more easily ensure that their costs keep to the average they think right). Others enjoy constantly trying out new recipes even though this makes costing harder. It may not be congenial to list the exact quantities you use in each dish, but it is essential for accurate costing – even at breakfast, you will need to know how many rashers, mushrooms, etc. per plate. For your guests' sake, as well as for your own costings, portions should not vary much in size (an electric slicer for meat is handy here and also speeds up service). Naturally, it is desirable to ask guests whether they want two eggs or one, a second helping of pudding, and so on – but for those who want more, there is always likely to be one who wants less.

SOURCES OF SUPPLY

If you want kitchen equipment to cater for largish numbers, it is worth getting from your newsagent some catering-trade papers where such things are advertised. You may pick up secondhand bargains as well (restaurants are constantly going bust). See Appendix for addresses of about a dozen specialised kitchen equipment shops, some of which have mail-order catalogues (see also your local Yellow Pages).

6.
Fuel and Energy

In its use of electricity, gas and other fuels, a guest-house is really just an ordinary home writ large. The activities that go on are like ordinary domestic ones, but they are conducted on a bigger scale: there are three-course meals to be prepared every night and cooked breakfasts every morning: a corresponding amount of washing up to be done; there is more laundering of bedlinen and towels; baths and washbasins will be in more frequest use (the cost of fuel for the last three items was estimated a few years ago at 50p per person per night); more rooms may have to be heated, perhaps to a higher level and for longer periods, than in a private house; and a greater number of people going in and out means more heat-loss through the front door.

Keeping bills low

All this involves energy, and increased fuel bills are an inevitable consequence of opening your house to guests. If you have recently done so and have kept your old bills, a comparison of consumption will be educational – compare units of fuel rather than sums of money. To do all you can to keep those bills down makes even more sense than for an ordinary householder, especially as fuel-saving measures often bring increased comfort and convenience as well as (sometimes rather than) economies.

Because of the sharp rises in fuel costs of some years ago, there is a vast amount of popular advisory literature around, much of it produced by the government as part of its Monergy campaign. Basic leaflets on insulation, heating systems, etc. are available free from the Energy Efficiency Office (Thames House South, Millbank, London SW1P 4QJ). A very thorough guide to all aspects of fuel economy is *Which Way to Cut Heating Bills* (Consumers' Association) – out of print but perhaps in your library – which would be well worth studying if you plan any but the most elementary measures. (The latter, which are the most cost-effective steps you can take, include such things as insulating your hot-water cylinder, rewashering dripping hot taps, and drawing all curtains just before it gets dark.)

Special economies

Information meant for the householder rather than someone running a business is all relevant, but the emphasis may be different. The following are some points of special importance to someone who runs a bed and breakfast house.

Thermostatic radiator valves, which control separately the temperature of each radiator to which one is fitted, are useful. They can automatically keep different rooms at different temperatures (bedrooms less warm than sitting-rooms, for example); they save on central heating costs in rooms where temperatures vary with the time of day (because of an open fire in the evening or sunshine in the morning); and if you close up some rooms in the winter, you can set the radiator valves just above the level at which condensation can start to cause trouble (10°C). It is important to tell each visitor how to adjust the temperature: otherwise, those who like cool bedrooms will simply fling open windows and send your fuel bill up.

Open fires are notoriously uneconomic of fuel, dusty, and work-making, but they are such a pleasure to guests that this consideration may outweigh their drawbacks. In particular, a wood fire is cheap and attractive. A stove for coal or wood, preferably with a glass front or one that can be opened, might be a good compromise.

Solid-fuel cookers (which, depending on their size, can also

63

provide hot water and central heating) are popular with many cooks, not least because they are so useful for real porridge cooked overnight, bread baking, and homemade yogurt. There are oil and gas equivalents, which create less dust and work.

Washbasins in bedrooms might be provided with a cold tap only and a wall-mounted instantaneous electric water heater to save plumbing costs (the Creda Corvette will give boiling water for tea, Redring make a very small version – either saves long lengths of hot water pipes running through the house).

Wall-mounted fan heaters are an economical and safe form of supplementary heating for bedrooms if central heating is insufficient, and one which guests are unlikely to leave on all night – unlike some heaters.

Electricity costs half as much at night if you have a special meter put in. Provided that there will be no disturbing noise, automatic washing-machines, tumble driers and dishwashers could operate then, and also other appliances – including cookers – controlled by time switches (portable switches can be bought). Electric heating on this system may be economic in some houses. Of particular interest when seeking to update an old building with the minimum of upheaval is the Electricity Council's free booklet *Total Heating*, about the latest ways of using cheap night-time electricity to provide daytime warmth and hot water. It also describes bedroom and bathroom heaters on automatic time controls for economy. (Obtainable from electricity boards.)

Loft insulation (which is nearly always worthwhile), tends to make bedrooms, rather than downstairs rooms, warmer. It is thus even more desirable in a bed and breakfast house than in an ordinary home.

Curtains, which should be thick or well lined, can be left closed in unused rooms during the winter. They are as effective as double glazing.

A freezer can be kept in an unheated outside building to cut running costs; keep it full, and open it as infrequently as possible.

Toasters in the dining-room will use less electricity than an electric grill in the kitchen (though the amount is small either way).

Fluorescent lamps cost about a third as much to run as filament bulbs giving the same amount of light, so consider them for areas which you have to light for long periods, such as passages, where their appearance is suitable.

Guests are unlikely to be considerate of your fuel costs: so fit door closers to prevent heat loss, and check each morning for dribbling hot taps, heaters left on, and so on. If contemplating an additional bathroom, consider a shower rather than a tub – three gallons of hot water rather than fifteen gallons each time it is used.

Ceilings can be lowered both to improve the proportions of a room, particularly where one big one has been divided, and to cut fuel costs by reducing the volume of air which has to be heated.

The heating system

When installing a new heating system or radically altering an existing one, it is important to use either a professional consultant or a well recommended and technically competent firm, as good design can save on both installation and running costs. You should also employ a firm that offers good maintenance and prompt emergency services to avoid embarrassing failure of the system. For the same reason, it is wise to have some grasp of how your system works.

Because you will be doing a lot of washing and washing up, it is better to have a boiler controller that times the hot water system separately from the central heating. Some controllers will switch different zones separately – the bedrooms and the living-rooms, for example.

7.
Official Approval

THE CROWN SCHEME

In 1987, a national scheme was introduced by the English Tourist Board under which all types of accommodation are classified. It is voluntary, and to be classified you have to pay a small annual fee. A Tourist Board officer should call each year to check your classification, which is not an assessment of quality but is based on the scale of facilities provided. This means that a very lovely house with perfect hosts and cordon bleu cooking might get a low classification simply because certain facilities (such as TV, or a sitting-room separate from the breakfast-room) were not available. There are houses with a high classification where, despite the provision of numerous facilities, ambience – that vital but indefinable quality – is all wrong; and, recognizing this, the Board is working on intended improvements to the scheme.

To get onto the lists of any regional Tourist Board is one way to secure visitors, and classification is a condition for taking a paid advertisement in certain official publications should you wish to do so. To obtain classification, it is necessary to satisfy at least the minimum standards, which are set out below. (For explanation of italics, see page 69.)

Bedrooms

1 *Internal lock, bolt or equivalent on bedroom door.*
2 Reasonable free space for movement and for easy access to beds, doors and drawers. Recommended minimum floor areas, excluding private bath or shower areas, are:
Single bedrooms – 60 sq ft (5.60m²)
Double bedrooms – 90 sq ft (8.40m²)
Twin bedded rooms – 110 sq ft (10.20m²)
Family rooms – 30 sq ft (2.80m²) – plus 60 sq ft (5.60m²) for each double bed – plus 40 sq ft (3.70m²) for each adult single bed – plus 20 sq ft (1.85m²) for each cot.
3 *Minimum bed sizes (except children's beds):*
Single beds – 6' × 2'6" (183 × 76 cm)
Double beds – 6' × 4' (183 × 122 cm).
4 Mattresses to be spring interior, foam or similar quality and in sound condition.
5 Bedding to be clean and in sufficient quantity.
6 Bed linen to be changed at least weekly and for every new guest.
7 *Bed linen other than nylon to be available on request.*
8 Beds to be made daily.
9 Bedrooms to be cleaned daily.
10 Clean hand towel to be provided for every new guest – changed as required.
11 Clean bath towels to be provided on request.
12 *Soap to be provided in rooms having wash-basins.*
13 At least one external window and adequate ventilation.
14 Opaque curtains or blinds on all windows.
15 Minimum lighting levels:
Single bedrooms – 100 watt or equivalent illumination.
Double bedrooms – 150 watt or equivalent illumination.
16 All bulbs, unless decorative, to have shades or covers.
17 Light to be controlled from the door.
18 Carpet or bedside rugs or mats.
19 Wardrobe or clothes hanging space with four hangers per person.
20 Dressing table or equivalent and mirror.
21 Bedside table or equivalent.

22 Adequate drawer space.
23 *One chair or equivalent.*
24 Waste paper container (non-flammable if smoking permitted).
25 Ashtray (where smoking permitted).
26 One drinking tumbler per guest.
27 Adequate heating according to season.

Bathrooms

1 *At least one bathroom, adequately ventilated and equipped with:*
  – bath or shower
  – wash handbasin and mirror (if any bedrooms without a wash handbasin)
  – electric razor point (if any bedrooms without razor point or adaptor available)
  – soap.
  Available at all reasonable times.
2 *At least one bathroom for every 15 resident guests (other than guests with private bathrooms or wash handbasin), available at all reasonable times.*
3 All bathrooms to be adequately heated.
4 Hot water at all reasonable times.
5 No extra charge for baths or showers.

WCs

1 *At least one WC, adequately ventilated, for every 12 resident guests (other than guests in bedrooms with private WC).*
2 Toilet paper and sanitary disposal bin in each WC.

General

1 Provision of breakfast.
2 Dining/breakfast-room (unless meals served only in bedrooms).

3 Public areas adequately lit for safety and comfort, with all bulbs, unless decorative, having shades or covers.
4 Adequate heating in public areas, according to season.
5 Public areas cleaned daily.
6 *Guests informed, when booking, if access to the establishment is restricted during the day.*

If each of your rooms satisfies these requirements, you can at least be listed by the Tourist Board; but if you want to apply for a superior classification (one, two, three or more crowns) the requirements are stricter, particularly in respect of items printed in italic on the above list. One crown criteria are all the requirements of the 'listed' category plus:

Bedrooms

1 *A lock to be fitted that will ensure privacy for guests and security for their property.*
2 Guests to be provided with the key to their bedrooms; duplicate or master keys being kept by the management.
3 *Minimum bed sizes (except children's beds):*
Single beds – 6'3" × 3' (190 × 90 cm)
Double beds – 6'3" × 4'6" (190 cm × 137 cm).
4 *Nylon bedlinen not acceptable.*
5 *Fresh soap for each new letting.*
6 Washbasin, (not wash-handbasin) e.g. adequate for a guest to wash hair, with hot and cold running water available at all reasonable times, either in the bedroom or in a private bathroom.
7 A light controlled from the bed.
8 Mirror, with light, above or adjacent to washbasin.
9 A 13 amp socket or suitable adaptor.
10 Electric razor point or adaptor available.
11 *One chair or equivalent per guest (minimum of two in family rooms).*
12 Heating without extra charge.
13 Resident guests permitted access to their bedrooms at all times.

Bathrooms

1 *At least one bathroom, equipped with a bath or shower for every 10 resident guests (other than guests in bedrooms with private bath or shower).*
2 At least one bathroom to be for the sole use of guests.
3 Access from bedrooms through public areas e.g. reception, lounge, etc., is not acceptable.

WCs

1 *At least one WC for every 8 resident guests, other than in bedrooms with private WC.*
2 *Where there is only one WC it must not be in a bathroom and must be for the sole use of resident guests.*
3 Access from bedrooms through public areas e.g. reception, lounge, etc., is not acceptable.

General

1 Reception facility, or bell to call for attention.
2 Lounge or foyer area(s) with adequate number of easy chairs.
3 Resident guests allowed access to lounge areas at all reasonable times.
4 Use of a telephone.
5 Tourist information available.

Items in italics are amendments to corresponding items in the lower classification.

Two crown criteria are all the requirements of one crown plus:

Bedrooms

1 Double beds to have bedside lights or a single bedhead light.

Single beds to have a bedside or bedhead light (twin beds may share a bedside light), in addition to a light controlled from the door.
2 All double beds to have access from both sides, with a bed-side table or equivalent for each person.
3 *Electric razor point (near a mirror).*

General

1 Dining/breakfast room normally separate from lounge (unless meals served only in bedrooms).
2 Early morning tea/coffee, served in bedrooms on request (unless beverage making facilities in bedrooms).
3 Hot beverages available on request in evening (unless beverage making facilities in bedrooms or nearby).
4 Early morning call, on request (or alarm clocks in bed-rooms).
5 Colour TV in lounge (if no TV available in all bedrooms and signal available).
6 Assistance with luggage on request.

  Again, in the lists above and below, items in italics are amendments to corresponding items in the lower classification.

Three crown criteria are all requirements of two crown plus:

Bedrooms

1 At least 33% of bedrooms to have a private bath or shower and WC en suite.
2 *One easy chair (plus one other chair if twin or double room).*
3 Full length mirror.
4 Luggage stand.
5 Fixed heating, having automatic and individual control.

General

1 Proprietor and/or staff available throughout the day.
2 A quiet lounge area, separate from a bar or TV lounge.
3 Automatically controlled fixed heating in public areas.
4 Shoe cleaning facilities.
5 Iron and ironing board available on request.
6 Hairdryers available on request.
    (Where Items 4, 5 and 6 are not provided in rooms, their availability should be advertised to guests).
7 *Public telephone – not exceeding BT rates.*

For four or five crowns even more is required; and in all categories, everyone is expected to observe high standards of courtesy, cleanliness, catering and service; to describe accurately what is offered; to allow visitors to look at bedrooms before booking, if they so wish; to make sure visitors know what extra charges there may be (VAT, service, tea, etc.), and to keep to quoted charges; to provide a bill or receipt if requested; and to deal promptly with enquiries and with complaints.

The scheme has now been extended to Scotland and Wales, but these have an additional system – not merely classifying but also 'grading' for quality. As in England, a 'crown' system is applied, but additionally a house may carry the accolade of being 'approved', 'commended' or 'highly commended' by grading officers of the relevant Tourist Board. This is a more subjective assessment involving criteria such as decor and friendliness. (This is why a bed and breakfast house might not display many crowns but still have a 'highly commended' plaque, which is awarded to only a few dozen establishments, including luxury hotels.) A similar system for England was under discussion at the time of writing.

THE MOTORING ORGANISATIONS

The Automobile Association applies its familiar system of stars only to hotels; guest-houses, private hotels, town and country homes (an Irish category), farmhouses and inns are merely 'listed'.

The AA's criteria for listing are broadly similar to the ETB's one crown standard, which means – among other things – that only houses in which all rooms have washbasins are eligible (except perhaps for farmhouses). There are minor differences: while the AA would apparently accept a windowless bedroom, the ETB would tolerate a shared table in the dining-room – but not vice versa! The more important ones are that the AA is slightly less demanding as to bathrooms (one per six *bedrooms*, compared to the ETB's one per ten *guests*, en suite facilities apart) and lavatories (one per six bedrooms compared to one per eight guests required by the ETB, which also requires that if there is only one w.c. it shall not be in a bathroom and must be for the sole use of guests). If only bed and breakfast is offered, the AA does not require a residents' sitting-room.

The AA has minimum numbers of bedrooms for different types of accommodation – guest-houses and private hotels (generally six), farmhouses (two), and inns (three), and there are special conditions for the last two. These minima mean that places which on all other grounds might be acceptable are excluded.

An inspection fee is payable to the AA on application for listing and an annual sum thereafter. A successful application means that your name appears in *Guesthouses, Farmhouses and Inns in Britain*, and that you can also buy advertising space in this. Otherwise, the main privilege of listing is that you can display the fact on your stationery and your premises.

The Royal Automobile Club, like the AA, awards stars to hotels only and 'lists' guest-houses, etc. The criteria used by the two organisations are similar, as are the privileges which come with acceptance. One difference is that the RAC will list a place with only three letting bedrooms, which the AA would generally reject. The RAC requires the option of a 'continental' breakfast to be offered.

The AA highlights in its guide those properties which it considers 'provide certain facilities or services which are of particular merit'. The RAC is more systematic, using 'acclaimed' and 'highly acclaimed' categories to indicate (principally) progressively larger and more comfortable bedrooms and higher percentages with en suite bathrooms – and those which have what the RAC calls 'an aura of luxury'.

The Michelin Guide includes guest-houses. Inspectors make unannounced visits and the organisers do not publish their criteria for inclusion. A condition of acceptance is that the house may not publicise the fact.

THE BRITISH TOURIST AUTHORITY

The British Tourist Authority, which is concerned with promotion overseas, has its own Commendation Schemes. These seek to promote the smaller country hotels, restaurants and guest-houses which offer their guests an 'outstanding welcome and excellent food, service and value for money'. Establishments apply to the BTA for commendation and plaques are awarded to successful applicants; all establishments are re-assessed annually. Commended establishments wishing to be marketed through the schemes are charged an initial application fee and successful establishments are charged an annual marketing fee. This covers a wide variety of marketing activity, including an entry in the annual guide *BTA Commended*, available free of charge through BTA offices overseas (and also on sale in Britain).

ACCOMMODATION DIRECTORIES

The AA, RAC and ETB inspections are pretty thorough (the AA spends £1 million a year to run its inspectorate) and the English Tourist Board sometimes uses AA inspectors to do their inspections for the crown classification scheme. The same cannot be said for all accommodation directories which claim to include only inspected accommodation. A guest-house proprietor reports of one organisation: 'Last year they asked me to inspect some properties in my area – about a 40-mile radius (for which I was paid £4 a visit – it didn't even start to pay for petrol). One of the houses which I visited, I told them was quite unsuitable, and it is still in the book this year.'

It does not do a house of high standard any good to be found listed alongside poor ones.

ADDRESSES OF APPROVALS AUTHORITIES

English Tourist Board and British Tourist Authority, Thames Tower, London W6 9EL.

Scottish Tourist Board, 23 Ravelston Terrace, Edinburgh, EH4 3EU.

Welsh Tourist Board, 2 Fitzalan Road, Cardiff, CF2 1UY. (This also issues 'Dragon' awards to guest-houses with certain facilities and whose owners have completed a course in guesthouse management.)

Northern Ireland Tourist Board, 48 High Street, Belfast, BT1 2DS.

Automobile Association, Fanum House, Basingstoke, RG21 2EA.

RAC, Lansdowne Road, Croydon, CR9 2JA.

8.

Getting Yourself Known

The length of this chapter is an indication of how important its subject matter is. It simply is not true that 'if a man write a better book or make a better mousetrap, though he build his house in the woods the world will make a beaten track to his door' (Emerson). The world has first to know that he and his house exist, and where.

PUBLICITY

Your publicity and selling effort is of prime importance. Redecoration and suchlike are essential too; but your redecoration will be seen by no one unless you give publicity efforts the priority they need – in winter and spring, for later may be too late.

Excellent bed and breakfast or guest-houses close down with sad regularity simply because too few visitors do make a track to their door. Here is the story of one, 'We made the great decision to leave London and start a new life doing something completely different. So we found our cottage and gave up our jobs, and sold our house (which took six months to complete), moved down in March 1983 and immediately started on renovating and decorating the cottage. That took six weeks working long hours, but we were determined to start bed and breakfast in May 1983. At first it was very slow, we advertised in two magazines but only got a few responses. We were relying on friends, colleagues, relatives and recommendations, and we took people off the road. We were so naive, we gave so much and charged so little. If my husband's company had not offered him a consultancy, we would not have been able to eat in the winter, all our savings having gone into the cottage and improvements.'

Advertising

The first thought of people new to the bed and breakfast business is to advertise, and as a result vast sums are thrown away every year. A small advertisement (too small to make its point among scores or hundreds just like it) is unlikely to do any good. A large one, very costly, may also be a failure. It is not the case that the big-circulation journals bring in big results, if they have the wrong sort of readership or if purchasers buy them to read articles and ignore the advertisements.

One proprietor may spend at the rate of £100 per bedroom; another £300 – but without getting three times as many bookings. But if you do decide to advertise, remember that the timing of any advertisement, and its position, are critical, as well as its wording – read others and try not to sound just like everybody else!

Here is an example of what I mean. There are three golden rules about any advertisement: first it should attract interest; then create desire; and finally stimulate action. Compare the two following examples advertising the same accommodation.

CLARIDGE HOUSE Porthloo, Cornwall	WHERE SPRING COMES EARLY
A warm welcome awaits you at our tastefully furnished house which is ideally situated. Good home cooking. We have spring interior mattresses and a fire certificate. Dogs not accepted. Prices on application. Tel. 012345678	Daffodils bloom in our clifftop garden and bedrooms have sea views. Local produce freshly cooked. Do come for an Easter break. £18 (half-board). Claridge House, Porthloo, Cornwall. Tel. 012345678

Which is more likely to catch readers' attention? Which is more likely to appeal to the sort of guests you want to attract? A little imagination can make all the difference.

For one bed and breakfast house to take a large advertising space – even in a county not a national newspaper – is uneconomic; but there may be a case for getting a few attractions in your area (not other bed and breakfast houses) to join with you and share both the space and the cost. Such an advertisement should show what makes it worthwhile to come to your area, a prerequisite to persuading anyone to stay at your house. The same principle of joint action could apply to direct mailings of several brochures in one envelope and with one covering letter. Subsidies for joint leaflets may be obtained from the Rural Development Commission, 11 Cowley St., London SW1P 3NA.

Every bed and breakfast owner is pestered with touts trying to sell advertising space or entries in directories. Many will be publications you have never heard of (nor has anyone else), or so-called special supplements featuring your area which are cobbled together merely as a vehicle for advertisements – a point patently obvious to readers who throw them away unread. Some directories never even get into print, and by the time they are due to appear the promoters (and your money) have vanished. The directories of the Tourist Boards and motoring organisations are, of course, entirely reputable: see chapter 6. And some people have had good results from advertising in the *Farm Holiday Guide* (see below) or the Yellow Pages. Business telephone subscribers are entitled to a free entry in the Yellow Pages, though their call charges are much higher than those for private subscribers. Yellow Pages are said to be much used by business travellers, though one proprietor found his inclusion brought him no guests but a lot of calls from sales representatives. You can even take advertising space on parking meters, if you feel that is the right place to be!

I have questioned several hundred bed and breakfast owners in the hope of finding a crock of gold – any publication in which advertisements invariably pull in bookings by the score. I have found *not one*.

If you do contemplate paying for an advertisement or entry, ask searching questions first. How many copies of the publication will be printed, and how many of those may actually be bought (judged on past performance)? Are these figures authenticated by the Audit Bureau of Circulation or just the publisher's say-so? Where will copies be sold? If given away, how and to whom? (A high proportion of give-aways are also thrown away – unread.) What is the quality of production like? Is anything known about the type of reader? How much space will you get for your money? What kind of reputation does the publication enjoy – is it influential or not? Unless its entries are backed by a high standard of inspection, you may find your house among a lot of inferior ones and that will do you no good at all. Haggle over the cost: you may get a discount for a first-time entry, for taking a series, etc. Accommodation guides which are really influential are now difficult to get into. Directories are put together as much as a year ahead, so book space in good time. You will have to decide your next year's prices well in advance: in the spring of the previous year.

While some publishers require payment with your order for advertising space, with or without a discount for early payment, others (principally official ones) invoice you nearer the date of publication or after. In this case, your money stays in your bank account for longer.

To get overseas visitors, you may find it pays to advertise in BTA's magazine *In Britain*, provided you are in a place that is known world-wide such as Bath.

If you have something to offer a very specific group of people (a trout stream for anglers is an example), then it may pay to advertise in a specialist magazine (on angling, in this case), provided you do so regularly, or in a specialist directory such as the Ramblers' Association's *Bed and Breakfast Guide*. One insertion will make little impact in a periodical.

A useful tip: if you join your local Women's Institute you will be entitled to a discount on any advertisements you place in their monthly, nationwide magazine.

Accommodation directories

Accommodation directories seem to be a better bet than newspapers or magazines. The *Farm Holiday Guides*, for instance (which cover more than farms) are annual paperbacks sold in bookshops, and they have a 40-year record. The volume for England, Wales and Ireland comprises about 3,000 advertisements: that for Scotland is much smaller. There is no inspection system and advertisers say whatever they want to about their houses. About 50,000 copies are printed. The publishers produce other accommodation guides, too: details from FHG Ltd, Abbey Mill, Seedhill, Paisley, PA1 1JN (telephone: 041-887 0428).

The BTA publishes accommodation directories for overseas visitors looking for farmhouse, inn or bed and breakfast accommodation. Among these is *Stay with a British Family,* of which some 35,000 copies are given away annually (abroad). You can expect to pay in the region of £50 for a short entry. This publication is for hosts who want to offer more personal hospitality than mere accommodation and food.

These are just two examples of many accommodation directories, and the only way to discover how effective any is for you is to try some out: don't, however, expect immediate results; and give each at least two tries, if you can, before you decide to give it up, because results vary inexplicably from year to year. In selecting which ones to use, study the standard of the houses featured in it – are they the kind with which you want yours to be associated? If the producers of the guide claim to inspect all houses featured, ask who does the inspecting and what are the criteria. 'Inspection' is a word that can mean much or little. Two ways to make your publicity more effective are to include a picture and quote your prices. And remember that selecting accommodation is more often done by wives than husbands. The cost of taking an entry in a resort's colour brochure is high – and even higher if it generates hundreds of requests for your own brochure with few of them resulting in bookings.

The task is going to be a long one, particularly if you are starting from scratch. It will be quite a time before the most potent (free) publicity of all takes effect: word-of-mouth recommendations by satisfied guests.

You need to set yourself an annual budget, and allocate it carefully – for instance, £100 per bed or 5 per cent of expected turnover – and not exceed it.

Distributing your brochure

Start locally, by equipping yourself with a really good card or brochure (see later). Before the season starts (February, a slack period, is a good month for this), take a supply to distribute personally to such useful contacts as the following and, in doing so, make yourself known to the staff who deal with the public – far more important to you than the top brass!

Several of the nearest Tourist Information Centres (list of addresses obtainable free from the English Tourist Board, Thames Tower, London W6 9EL) and also Citizens' Advice Bureaux.

Local vicars and even undertakers (because people attending weddings and funerals may need accommodation), doctors and solicitors.

Hospitals (the medical social worker may need to help visiting relatives to find rooms).

Any local boarding schools or colleges (they may need accommodation for visiting parents, particularly if they hold open days or the like, for temporary staff or for visiting lecturers).

Establishments similar to your own but in other parts of the country, if you know that their facilities and standards are comparable (riders will want to try other places near stables, people who have enjoyed staying on an arable farm may want to try a hill farm, and so on).

Estate agents (house-hunters from distant parts may need rooms).

Antique and craft shops (where tourists may ask for advice on where to stay).

Pubs, garages, restaurants and cafés, car hire firms, airport accommodation desk, railway station, taxi drivers.

Large companies likely to have business visitors: a hard foot-slog round the nearest industrial estate worked wonders for one Oxfordshire bed and breakfast owner. Ask to see the managing director's secretary, as it is often left to secretaries to make reservations.

Tourism officers in town or county halls, local chambers of commerce and tourism associations.

Kiosks in national parks and information desks in stately homes, wildlife parks, historic monuments and other sights are often willing to pin up cards.

81

Police stations keep lists of bed and breakfast houses for the use of stranded travellers and the like.

Pay to have a card permanently in every newsagent's window within, say, a 10-mile radius of your house; and ask local hotels and even other guest-houses to send on to you any enquiries they cannot accommodate themselves (and offer to reciprocate). (But your standards will have to be similar and your prices comparable – the arrangement may come to an abrupt end if the other place finds that you are giving better value!) Finally, re-read chapter 1 and you will get more ideas about people to approach.

Always carry a few brochures on you and in your car, to hand to anyone interested, and with you on holiday (in Britain or abroad). If non-residents frequent your premises (for meals perhaps), lay brochures out for them to take. At a Perthshire hotel, putting out supplies of their very attractive accommodation brochures in their bar results in about 3,000 a year being taken by people who come for meals (as well as residents): as a result, they have had guests arrive from America, Australia and many other places, clutching a brochure given to them by a friend.

If you think it worth while, you can send 100 copies to the British Tourist Authority's circulation unit for free overseas distribution (it is at 4 Bromells Road, London SW4 0BJ); and for a small fee BTA will take 1,000 for display in its big Travel Centre (12 Regent Street, Piccadilly Circus, London SW1Y 4PQ).

Where the local Tourist Information Centre is concerned, it is worth backing up your supply of brochures by phoning once or twice a week to report the number of vacancies you have, which will remind the staff of your existence and give you a chance to find out whether their stock of your brochure needs replenishing.

Direct mail

If you do not want to call personally (which is preferable, as you may then learn more about what needs there are to be filled), you can post your brochures with covering letters. It is not good to send photocopied circulars: a personal-seeming letter is much better, and this effect can be inexpensively achieved by having it typed on a word-processor. The main part of the text is repeated automatically in every letter but the recipient's name and address are typed in individually (and the opening paragraph can be varied to suit different recipients). Shop around for someone to do the word-processing, as charges (and competence) vary a lot (see Appendix).

Sending a circular to potential new visitors is worth considering if you can obtain a list of likely people. For instance, systematically studying the 'engagements' column in your local paper is worthwhile. You can then write to fiancées offering accommodation for guests attending their weddings later. Or you might think 'retired teachers' a good group to choose: and in one particular part of the country, perhaps the affluent southeast (study the addresses in your visitors' book)? But consider the cost of this exercise. There are companies that make a living by compiling lists of this type, but you would have to pay £50 or more for the use of a list of 1,000 names – it is hardly worth mailing fewer, for you may be lucky to get one in a hundred replying – to which must be added the cost of whatever letter and/or brochure you send out. (The Post Office may offer you a special deal if you have never used direct mail before, wanting to encourage new people to try this medium.) Alternatively, you can address envelopes from directories (e.g. of doctors, clergy or whatever) held in public libraries, at no cost but some effort. The Post Office will also distribute circulars through all letterboxes in a given area for a fee that is much cheaper than posting them to varied addresses. If you have had one contented visitor from (say) Fitzjohns Avenue, Hampstead, would such a circular to every house in that avenue produce results? More information is available from the Post Office Direct Mail Department (see Appendix).

Passing trade

If you are on a road, a bed and breakfast sign can, without the expense of advertising, bring in visitors if you want passing trade. When you do not want any, a 'no vacancies' sign can be hooked onto it – preferable to announcing 'vacancies' which looks as if you are not popular, and which makes it difficult to turn away any caller whom you do not like). If you are not on a fairly busy road, signs at the nearest junctions will help. Remember that signs not on your own property require not just the agreement of the landowner, but planning permission, which you may not get. National Park authorities are particularly strict. One Lake District guest-house at the end of a dale lost nearly all its trade when forced to remove a directional sign from the road at the entrance to the dale. In some counties, large guest-houses may apply for an official sign at a distance, directing casual visitors to the house but not naming it. If you offer accommodation to guests who have not booked in advance, and you have at least four bedrooms or eight beds, you have to display in a prominent place maximum and minimum overnight charges and what guests receive for them (bath, meals, etc.) including VAT.

Booking services

There exist a number of booking services, which, in return for a fee and/or commission, say they will obtain bookings for you. Usually the money asked is very substantial, with no guarantee or results. Be on your guard against any that try to tie you to them exclusively, while not assuring you of any bookings.

The AA runs a Wayfarers scheme for accommodating overseas visitors (details from the AA, Fanum House, Basingstoke, RG21 2EA). Travellers buy a set of vouchers with which to pay for rooms, booking into houses from the Wayfarer list as they tour along – they do not book ahead but at a day's notice only. (This means Wayfarer travellers fill up rooms which otherwise would probably stay empty.) For each voucher the proprietor sends back to the AA, he or she gets a fixed sum less 2% to pay for the AA's work. He or she can charge visitors extra for private bathrooms, dinner, etc.; but not for making a phone call to do the next night's booking for them.

A bed and breakfast scheme to help both proprietors and Oxfam is run by Rosemary Schlee (tel. 03943 2740). She keeps a register of proprietors, mainly in East Anglia, who have agreed to donate one third of their bed and breakfast charges to Oxfam. She does all the publicity that brings in the visitors; and when these phone her she passes them on to those houses in her scheme which have vacancies on the relevant dates. When guests pay at the end of their stay, they are handed a receipt for the one-third which will go to Oxfam.

Bed and Breakfast (GB) is a reservation service for overseas visitors which has BTA's official backing. One of its advantages to participants is that they get paid in advance and in sterling. Membership currently costs £52.50 (much less if you make a two-year commitment; nil to London houses) with a small percentage for each booking made – there is a scale which ranges from 5% to 11%. The agency reserves the right to inspect if it wishes but does not do so automatically. Its address is Box 656, Henley-on-Thames, RG9 1XS; tel. 0491 578803.

A rather different type of service is provided by many Tourist Information Centres. If you keep them frequently informed of vacancies, they will pass on travellers who apply to them for accommodation. They may take a commission in the form of a 10 per cent deposit (for one night), paid to them by the visitor.

Reservation services are much used by London bed and breakfast houses in particular, who pay perhaps 10% to have visitors sent to them: usually bookings are made on the same day and are therefore useful for filling rooms still vacant. Most of these services are listed in *How to Book Accommodation*, free from the British Tourist Authority. Some ferry companies and airlines also run booking services.

Travel agents

If you want overseas visitors, it may be worth sending your brochure to what are called 'incoming operators': people who handle accommodation (and other) arrangements for overseas visitors once they get here. Some take visitors around in large groups which need large hotels, but a number specialise in individual clients (they may even take them around in cars). BTA publishes a list of 300. A high standard of accommodation is expected. BTA also knows which overseas operators are interested in booking their clients into small bed and breakfast houses. The ports of entry on the east coast of England receive many enquiries from visitors who have come across on ferries with a view to touring round England: sending each one six of your brochures might be worthwhile, with a letter asking if they would like more.

Getting repeat business

Another way to spread your name is to have a really good picture postcard of your house on sale to visitors (at a lower price than postcards of local views) for them to send to friends, making sure that in small type on the back are your address, phone number and a few tempting details. The same picture may do for Christmas cards to send to visitors who might return again if reminded of your existence.

Some houses find that, in securing repeat bookings, the despatch (in February) of a circular letter to previous visitors is effective, particularly if there is news to relate – for instance, improved facilities, redecoration, family news, a special offer to returning guests and/or to friends they recommend. Always write as you speak – no business jargon or advertisement-style 'hype'.

Penscot (Somerset) does this. A lively and well written circular sent to 300 past visitors each January results in a 50% response (bookings) by the end of August, and more sub-sequently. 'We go through our card index of visitors to pick the 300, a big job,' says Tony Tilden. 'but as a result we have cut out nearly all our previous advertising.'

Offering a discount on a next-year booking to those staying with you this year, provided they book ahead (and pay a deposit), is another way to secure repeat business from satisfied customers. For this purpose you could use vouchers worded as follows:

> This voucher is worth £5 if
> presented at _____
> when paying for a visit of
> three days or more, within
> twelve months of _____
>   (date)

When visitors do come back, how useful it will be if you have a card index on which you can look up details of their previous visit – from their children's names to their food preferences. To be remembered on returning is something that will really impress your visitors.

Responding to enquiries

Whatever you do, it is going to be a hard and unremitting slog; and some owners report that, of every 10 to 15 people who get as far as making an enquiry, only one actually books (even when they already know prices, etc. from a directory). Your brochure may be much more effective if you also enclose some leaflets about local sights and the attractions of the area; free supplies can be obtained from your nearest Tourist Information Centre.

All these efforts will be wasted if you are careless about the follow-up. If telephone enquiries result, will there always be someone at home to answer the phone (or an answering machine)? When enquiries arrive by post, will you answer them the same day, and have you always got an ample stock of brochures (not to mention stationery and stamps) at the ready? Incredibly, one can telephone for prices and be told, 'I'm not sure'! There are plenty of other places to which your potential visitors can go if you fumble or delay. The Home-sitters agency provides live-in people to answer your phone and caretake when you're away: telephone 0296 631289 for details.

The press

Editorial publicity in newspapers and magazines is very valuable, and it costs you more in effort than in money. It is more likely to be read than any advertisement, and it carries greater weight. But obtaining it is not easy unless you know the ways of the publishing word. (The fees a publicity consultant would charge are unlikely to be economic.)

If yours is just another bed and breakfast house, even if you are sure it is the best in the country, then you will have little to interest the press. But if there is anything at all different about the premises – like one in Northumberland, which is built of stone from Hadrian's Wall – then you may catch a journalist's attention. If you offer more than basic accommodation and catering – craft tuition, pony trekking, musical evenings – either usually or on occasion, the same is true.

How to get press publicity? The English Tourist Board and some regional Tourist Boards produce regular bulletins of news which they send to the press, in which you might be included: make contact with the person responsible for press relations on the staff of your Tourist Board (assuming you are a member). You could also act on your own initiative by finding *Willing's Press Guide* in your public library and looking up all special-interest magazines whose readers might like what you have to offer – those for riders, anglers, wildlife enthusiasts, the elderly, music-lovers and so on. Then send each a brochure (another reason for having a prepossessing and informative one), with the relevant features of your house picked out with a highlighter pen or by some such means. Never attempt to provide a write-up composed by yourself, simply supply facts. You might care to offer a local paper or radio station a free weekend for two for them to offer to readers/listeners as a prize in a competition, provided you get good publicity in return.

For this and other purposes, it is well worth having good photographs of your house, as there is a chance of one being used to illustrate an article. These should be taken by a professional or an expert amateur: shaky snapshots and Polaroids are useless. Have a few colour prints and black-and-white enlargements on hand.

The chore of envelope addressing can be done during the slack period of late autumn. Monthly magazines are prepared well in advance, and it is the spring and summer issues that you will probably want to get into. Send information on special events and Christmas houseparties correspondingly early. Both information and photographs will often be filed by magazines for future use.

An approach to a magazine may result in no more than a telephone call from an advertising salesperson wanting your money. Do not be talked into taking advertising unless perhaps you want to follow up an editorial mention with a reminder in the next issue. Have no truck with any periodical that promises you editorial publicity in return for buying space.

You may think that local publicity is not worthwhile because visitors come from far afield. But it has its uses. Half the holiday trips made in this country by the British are to visit friends or relations; not all want to stay in their houses. As already mentioned, local businesses sometimes have to find accommodation for their visitors. Getting free local publicity is not too difficult if you can find, or contrive, something special to make your house newsworthy – winning an award (like a BTA commendation; see chapter 6) or cooking a special menu, perhaps reviving historic local recipes. As well as the local and county newspapers or magazines, think about local radio, hospital radio services, student magazines, and church magazines.

You might get yourself valuable free publicity in an influential national newspaper or magazine if you are willing to offer a travel writer (and spouse) a free weekend, in conjunction with some tourist attraction that is really unusual and interesting in your area – sufficiently unusual to tempt the writer to come, which it is unlikely your house alone could do (travel writers are inundated with invitations to all parts of the globe). But beware of one thing. If a mass-circulation magazine stimulates huge numbers of readers to write to you for brochures, this will cost you a fortune and may not bring enough actual bookings to compensate. Therefore, try to ensure that any mention of your house says 'To book, telephone . . .'. You may get a better response from freelance writers (each of whom writes for many publications) than from writers on the staffs of newspapers: the former get fewer invitations and expenses-paid trips. Addresses of many are in the membership list of the British Guild of Travel Writers (for current price of this, telephone 01-998 2223.)

Some people are better than others at publicising their own activities – it is largely a matter of temperament. If you feel happy to do so, try serving on committees of your local tourism association; give talks to Women's Institutes and the like on running a bed and breakfast house; volunteer to help man the local Tourist Information Centre; join local clubs and societies to help increase your network of useful contacts . . . but not if your time could be more usefully spent back at the house.

A useful free book is *The Small Businessman's Guide to the Media* from Thomson Directories, Freepost, Farnborough, GU14 7BR.

Once it becomes known that you are a bed and breakfast house, you will be pestered by touts trying to get money and/or free accommodation on one pretext or another. Here are two examples. A proprietor received a letter from an unknown woman claiming to be compiling an accommodation guide (no title stated and no publisher named): could she have a free dinner, bed and breakfast in return for the ensuing publicity?

Answer – a firm 'no'. But how many suckers said 'yes', thus providing a free round-Britain trip for this lady? Second example: a periodical from a religious-sounding organisation telephoned proprietors soliciting advertisements. 'Let me see your publication first,' one replied. What he got instead was an invoice for over £60, for advertising space booked for his house. 'Not interested', he wrote on the invoice before posting it back. Nevertheless, an advertisement appeared, and further invoices followed.

'I am a journalist writing about . . .' 'I am a market researcher conducting a survey on . . .': these are some of the spurious claims made by people who phone (or, less usually, write) out of the blue, and whose real intention is to exploit you. Beware, too, of 'directories' in which you can be listed – for a fee. Some of them never get published; or not in any quantity to do you any good.

THE BROCHURE

'I'm too small to need a brochure,' some say. But a small house can find that having even the simplest of brochures increases bookings, if it is well conceived, and it saves some letter-writing.

In fact, keeping a brochure simple (and inexpensive) is important. If you go in for anything elaborate, such as full-colour printing, the cost per brochure will be very high on small quantities, and large quantities are undesirable as you may want to update the information before long.

Your brochure exists to persuade people that your house, and its area, are so attractive that they will want to come and stay. A picture of the house on the front is almost an essential; and probably a good drawing will do it more justice than a grey photograph. Photographs have to be exceptionally clear and crisp to reproduce well, and they have to be printed on some-what shiny paper which often looks a bit cheap and nasty but in fact is quite expensive: the worst of both worlds. (An alternative is to have prints of a colour photograph done and then stick these on yourself by hand; but this, too, is costly – and laborious. Some firms supply small prints with self-adhesive backs (see Appendix).) There is occasionally a case for an aerial photograph, but the cost is high. An alternative is a photograph taken from the top of a telegraphic mast (see Appendix).

Amateurish drawings give a poor impression, so if you do not know an artist or draughtsman, ask advice from your local college of art or the art teacher at a school. A printer may also be able to help, and the availability of advice on illustration and layout may help you decide which printer to use (see below).

Think also of including more than just a picture of the front of the house. If you are particularly proud of your sitting- or dining-room, or of your garden, consider an extra picture. The view from the rooms, though important to visitors, is rarely shown in brochures but might be worth considering. Such additional illustrations can be smaller than the main one; they must each have a brief caption.

Essential information

The full address of your house should be given (with postcode), telephone number and dialling code, and your own name. And remember that although you know where your house is, the enquirer does not, so some guidance is essential. If your house is conspicuous and easy to find, a few words will suffice: e.g. 'Opposite church in High Street', 'Two miles from Barchester on A999 towards Ambridge'. But if it is deep in the country or in a back street, a simple map or plan is advisable, perhaps on the back of the brochure. (This might indicate such useful features as motorway, mainline railway, or airport, too.)

You may also want to relate your address to some town the user can identify or to a major attraction: e.g. 'Two miles north of Oxford'. Do not use a diagram drawn from memory, with side-turnings omitted and the scale all wrong, for an inaccurate map is worse than none, resulting in late arrivals of cross visitors who lost their way. Trace the roads from a proper map, then put in whatever place-names, landmarks or road numbers you think will be helpful. Better still, leave this work to a professional draughtsman.

Describing your house

The hardest part is to write the description of your house in a way that will give the reader a really clear idea of what it is like. Is it a historic building? Does it have a ghost? Has it an attractive garden or landscape around it? (If not, what are its surroundings?) A large garden is well worth mentioning. Do not use meaningless platitudes like 'tastefully furnished, 'a warm welcome awaits you', 'good home cooking', 'spring-interior mattresses', etc. – so many other houses (good and bad) use the same phrases, and in any case no enquirer expects ugly furniture, hostile hosts, bad food and lumpy beds to be on offer! It is rather doubtful whether anyone is impressed by being told that you have got a fire certificate (compulsory for all but the smallest houses) or belong to the town's tourist association or suchlike (merely meaning you subscribe). As to other commendations, see chapter 6.

It is certainly worth finding space to mention any official approbation your surroundings may have received. For example, in a town, that your house is in a conservation area; or, in the country, that it is in an official area of outstanding natural beauty; or, by the sea, that the nearest beach is one of the scandalously few unpolluted ones (list, £2, from the Coastal Anti-Pollution League, 94 Greenway Lane, Alverstoke, Bath, BA2 4LN). Similarly, is your house a listed building? If so, say so. Try to give the reader an idea of your own particular style. Can you, for instance, say the rooms are furnished with antiques or Laura Ashley fabrics or give some other specific description? If you serve dinner, then print details of the kind of food you serve. Either say 'A typical menu may comprise . . .' or list some of the dishes you regularly serve, so that people know whether your style of cooking is of the stewed steak and shepherd's pie kind or runs to cordon bleu dishes. Say how many courses the meal comprises and whether coffee is extra. If you serve it unusually early (6.30) or late (8.00), say so, and also if there are days of the week when you do not serve dinner. Mention how many bedrooms you have, and other rooms available to visitors, as this gives an idea of how many people a visitor will meet. Are dining-tables separate or shared? Do you dine with your guests?

Think out what extra features or services you offer which many other houses do not. If people read that you change towels daily, offer free tea on arrival, bake your own bread, have log fires, etc., they get a picture of attentive hosts with high standards. The provision of central heating, TV, adequate bathrooms and so forth are also things visitors want to know about.

93

State limitations, too, to save later misunderstandings or disappointments. This includes making it clear whether or not it is all right to bring children, a dog or a handicapped person. How accessible are you by public transport?

Selling the locality

Remember that you have to 'sell' not only your house but your area too, so describe briefly the local scenery and list some of the local sights (stately homes, museums, wildlife parks, etc.). If the area has possibilities for walkers, golfers, anglers, birdwatchers, etc., say so. Don't, on the other hand, go too far in emphasising that it is within a day's drive of half-a-dozen famous tourist centres like Bath, Stratford-on-Avon, etc.: you risk putting your visitor off your area if you give the impression that anything worth seeing is at some distance from it.

Printing and paper

Obtain (from Tourist Information Centres, etc.) brochures of other bed and breakfast or guest-houses, and study their good and bad points. Write out all the points you wish to make (on separate sheets – front cover, inside pages, back cover), and sketch a map with details of how to find you.

Visit more than one printer to find out what services they can offer and how helpful they seem, to obtain rough quotations, and to see comparable jobs they have done. Printers' names can be obtained from Yellow Pages; your regional Tourist Board or your local paper may help. But make a few decisions first, related to how you intend to use your brochures.

If you intend to distribute them widely, or expect to have a lot of enquiries, you will want to economise. If you plan to be more selective, then the cost per copy can be higher (though costs of any printing job fall sharply with numbers). Stout opaque paper is essential (but not heavy if you plan to send any overseas, because of postage costs); very fancy card or paper is not.

The shape should be a standard one, so that it will fit into a standard size of envelope (white, not cheap brown manilla) and be economical to print. A good one is one-third A4 (about 8 ¼ " by 4"), or a larger sheet folded to this size: it is widely used for tourist literature and will fit the racks used in most Tourist Information Centres, if you intend to use these (in which case the brochure should be printed vertically and be stiff enough to stay upright).

Either tinted paper or coloured ink (which should be very dark, especially for pictures and maps) looks pleasant, but both used together make for hard reading.

The tariff

Where your tariff is concerned, this may be better printed on a separate slip, changed annually. This information could be quite lengthy if you charge different prices for different rooms or at different seasons. Do you intend to make a surcharge for one-night stops, or discounts for long stays? Bargain breaks in winter? What will you charge a single person who occupies a double room? Children's rates? Dogs? If you charge extra for (e.g.) bedroom tea facilities, flasks of tea, or anything else, this should be stated. This is the place, too, to say when you will be closed, and whether or not you take people at Christmas. Prices should be inclusive of VAT and of service (though you can say that gratuities to any staff are at visitors' discretion). This slip is the place to go into detail about the exact number of rooms and which have (for example) twin beds, washbasins, or en suite bathroom.

These inserts can be printed more cheaply on thinner paper, so that if you make alterations to your house or to your prices, you can reprint without having to do the entire brochure. This will make it possible to put more money into the brochure and have an economic quantity printed, as it will not become obsolete.

Part of this slip can be a booking form. This should incorporate spaces for the following information:

Name (in capitals)
Address (with postcode)
Phone number
Date of arrival, with alternative
Date of departure, with alternative
Number of adults
Number of children and their ages
Bedrooms required (single, twin, double, family)
Meals required (bed & breakfast, or dinner, bed & breakfast)
Special requirements such as: cot, private bath,
    accommodation for dog, special diet
The total deposit enclosed (the rate of deposit should be
    stated).

You could also add the question 'Where did you hear of us?', later analysing all the answers to see which of your publicity measures pay off and which do not. This is also the place to print any booking conditions – e.g. date by which deposit must be received, liability in the event of cancellation, rules regarding dogs, latest time for arriving or departing.

Cards

You may find it a good idea to have in addition a small card, with a picture and a minimum of information, for wider distribution: for instance, to give quantities to local pubs, shops and petrol stations who may get members of the public asking where they can find a bed, and to display in newsagents' windows (that is, if you want casual trade of this kind). Give one, or a brochure, to each departing guest in the hope that they will want to get in touch with you again or will pass it on to a friend.

9.

Making Your Visitors Happy

This is, after all, what the whole thing is about!

FIRST IMPRESSIONS

It begins even before you have met your guest. He phones or writes for information, or to book – if he does not get a prompt response, and a cordial one, you may never hear of him again. He may have particular requirements which you cannot meet, or do not want to; all the more need to say so courteously, and with regret, to temper his disappointment. An experience like asking whether a firm mattress is available, and being told curtly, '*My* mattresses are soft and perfectly comfortable' expresses a snubbing, take-it-or-leave-it attitude which imme-diately demonstrates that one would be wiser to stay elsewhere. You may have rules you want to enforce, but there are different ways of setting about this. A terse 'no children' sounds hostile; how much better to say, 'We're sorry but our house is not suit-able for children.' In everything you say or do, you are express-ing your personality and, if you give an unfortunate impression (that includes pretentious behaviour – such as menus written in French), guests will be extra critical from then on and not return. Above all, never say 'don't'! There are other ways to get your message across, like, for instance, the following notice which appears on every lavatory in a house in Dorset:

Our drainage system is on a strict diet
and is expressly forbidden to consume
Kleenex, cigarette ends, yesterday's
picnic remains, teabags or any manufactured
article except loo paper. Please put all
such things in the pedal-bin provided.
Thank you!

Writing to guests

When writing to a guest, your letter will sound pleasanter if you begin 'Dear Mr So-and-so' (never 'Dear Sir') and sign it 'Yours sincerely, John Brown' (not 'J. Brown'), because you are in a business where a friendly and not a formal mode is appropriate. The more trouble you take over your written style, the more favourable may be the effect; and it is worth giving time and thought to this. For instance, visitors booking into Tregynon, a farmhouse in Wales, receive with the slip confirming their booking a letter of welcome which must make recipients impatient to set off there at once!

'As you have not stayed with us before you may like to know more about us. Essentially, we are a small family team consisting of myself, Peter, my wife, Sheila, and our two children Philip and Anita.

Having suffered some 17 years of the 'rat-race' in London, we decided to change our lives and bought this house in March 1980. The next two years were spent renovating the farmhouse whilst at the same time building up both the livestock and catering side of the business . . .

We have no doubts that the beauty of the surrounding unspoilt countryside with its abundance of wildlife will play its part. The weather we can do little about, though surprisingly for Wales, this stretch of coast is near the top of the sunshine table for the U.K. as a whole.

The rest, therefore, is down to us and, in particular, Sheila, who is responsible for masterminding operations in the kitchen. In this respect, you may like to know that whenever possible we use fresh food from our own holding, including free-range eggs, cheese, trout, vegetables, etc. We even have our own 'smoke-house' on the premises where we oak-smoke bacon and gammon in the traditional manner. Virtually everything on the menu is home-made and, as far as possible, we avoid the use of produce containing artificial additives and preservatives.

Our range of speciality breads and rolls (made exclusively for us to our specifications by the master baker in Newport) are free from any additives and animal products. We have 100% rye breads for those on wheat-free diets and gluten-free loaves for coeliacs.

Our breakfast sausages are made for us to our own recipe and contain nothing other than meat, cereal and spices.

We have also commissioned a renowned local cheesemaker to produce a vegetarian version of his now famous organic farmhouse cheese.

Many of these products are for sale and we can also arrange an ongoing mail-order service for certain items. We should, however, be grateful for as much notice as possible should you wish to take home some of these 'goodies'.

Meal times are as flexible as we are able to make them but we do like to serve children's meals to our younger guests between 5.30 p.m. and 6.30 p.m. Reductions are made for meals taken at these times.

Parents are particularly asked to respect the enjoyment that peace and tranquillity can bring to others and to ensure, as far as possible, that any children in their care who are unable to appreciate this, vacate the lounge and dining-room by 7.15 p.m.'

Arrival and registration

A good host or hostess will be prompt in answering the door to an arriving guest, will greet him or her with a smile and help to carry luggage up. The entrance hall creates a lasting first impression: let it be light, attractively furnished, free of family raincoats and brollies, with flowers, and without a plethora of do-and-don't notices. Offer tea (this is usually free – make it clear if it is not) and show the visitor where bathroom, sitting-room and dining-room are. Either now or later the visitor should sign the registration book or form.

Even if you let only one bedroom, you are required by law (the Hotel Records Order 1972) to record certain information about your visitors, whether they are foreign or British, namely: address, nationality, passport number (if applicable), and next destination. Police may inspect to check that you are doing this.

It can also be useful to you to have some other details. For instance: car number – in case the car is obstructing something, in case you want to check whether the visitor is in or not, and – rarely, one hopes – in case he departs without paying and you want the police to locate him; and intended method of payment – in case a period for cheque clearance is needed.

All this is simple if you have registration forms for visitors to fill in like the one illustrated on page 101.

Compliments and complaints

In due course it is important to make time to chat, particularly about your area and its points of interest or the history of your house if it is old, and to introduce guests to one another (unless it is clear that one wants to keep himself to himself). If you have a hobby, such as spinning or patchwork, your visitor may be interested to see how you do it. Always ask whether a guest needs more of anything (from pillows to food) and whether everything is to his or her satisfaction. You should enjoy the resulting compliments, and be able to learn from any criticisms, though the nicer people are, the less likely they are to voice the latter, unfortunately. Unless told, you may remain unaware of discomforts which could be easily rectified but could lose you repeat business. Noise is one: rumbling plumbing or gurgling radiators, a loud extractor fan, a dog that barks at night, early milk deliveries, noisy late guests, kitchen clatter, family arguments or radio, thin walls.

Even in the best run house, there will be guests who have cause for complaint, real or imagined. The way it is dealt with is in many cases much more important than the complaint itself: a dismissive attitude or a defensive one only makes matters worse. It is extremely hard to deal tactfully with a complaint you believe unfounded, but sooner or later this situation will turn up, and if you mishandle the incident it will certainly escalate. I have analysed a number of letters of complaint about various bed and breakfast houses, and have come to the conclusion that very few I have seen were wholly justified – but behind each there often lay the same sequence of events: at the outset, some offputting incident (perhaps quite minor) which got things

Full name (*capitals*) _____

Address _____

_____

_____

Phone No. _____ Car No. _____

Nationality _____ Number in party _____

Date of arrival _____

Date of departure _____

Intended method of payment:
  Cash / cheque (sterling) / traveller's cheque / other:

How did you originally hear of us?

Passport No. _____

Issued at _____

Next destination (*address*)

off to a bad start (particularly if the host was not able to put this right straight away), so that from then on the visitor, consciously or unconsciously, began looking for other things to grumble about. Perhaps on arrival the bath water is cold. The tired and chilly new arrival comes downstairs unbathed and in an edgy temper. If then the duck is a little underdone, the television on the blink or the coffee less than piping hot his aggravation multiplies. It is a curious phenomenon that discontented guests rarely voice their criticisms there and then – giving the host a chance to bring another dish, attend to the television fault or make fresh coffee – but often go away and complain bitterly where they think it will do most damage. Therefore it is important for hosts to *ask* their guests whether they are finding everything to their satisfaction: far, far better to know what is causing discontent than, ostrich-like, to assume that 'no complaints' means no causes for complaint.

You may be used as the target for visitors' own bad feelings. Example: Husband and wife quarrel in the car. Wife, soon after arrival and still distracted, lets bath overflow. She feels she is now in your bad books too. By then criticising your food, your house, your service, she subconsciously tries to get her husband back on her side against the common 'enemy', you – and quite probably succeeds. If things go from bad to worse, they later write a malicious letter to the Tourist Board or suchlike saying you should not be recommended.

All very upsetting -- unless you remember that every house sooner or later has such an incident; and that Tourist Boards know that a number of complaints have a malicious motive.

INDUCEMENTS TO RETURN

Apart from ensuring that your guests are at ease with you, and comfortable in your home, there is a third, vital, element to their stay which in my experience is largely overlooked by perhaps nine out of ten bed and breakfast houses. It is this. Tourists who come to you are not coming primarily because they want to stay in your house: they come because they want to be in (or pass through) your part of the country. And yet I consistently find bed and breakfast houses badly lacking in information to give a visitor which will demonstrate that theirs is an area worth lingering in, or returning to. An untidy heap of miscellaneous and out-of-date brochures in some unlit corner is the most that is usually available.

Overnight visitors

Every bed and breakfast proprietor complains about one-nighters, hurrying on to the next place on their tour. They create a lot of work (changing bedlinen in particular). Hosts never get to know these visitors, nor do the visitors get to know the area. However, what proprietors – if they are imaginative – often achieve from the one-nighters is a return visit for a much longer stay, provided they come to realise that the area is interesting enough to deserve further exploration.

Tourist information

The presentation of tourist information is crucial: it is what has often caused a family who booked in for only one night to stay on or return, for as much as a week or more, when once they realised how much there was to see and do. This happens all the time, especially in little-known but attractive places that are used as stopovers on the way to better-known destinations like Scotland or the west country.

Here are ways to set about this, which you may like to consider.

1 Before Easter, take a trip to the nearest town's Tourist Information Centre and get a supply of the scores of leaflets they have, publicising local 'sights'.
2 Buy, for each bedroom, (or at least for the sitting-room) an album with transparent plastic sleeves and fill it with a set of the leaflets. (The owner of a particularly elegant bed and breakfast house in Essex covers large detergent cartons in

pretty wallpapers and fills each with an assortment of tourist leaflets for visitors to browse through.)

3 Alternatively, make or buy a large wall-rack (wood or wire) to contain stocks of the leaflets, from which visitors can help themselves. (You may or may not have wall-space, and you will have to keep replenishing exhausted stocks). One thing not to do is dump the leaflets in what will inevitably become an untidy pile on a table. Some 'sights' produce, as well as expendable leaflets, small posters (A4 size). If you wish to display these, an area of wall covered with cork tiles is a good way to do so.

4 Obtain a large-scale (e.g. 1:50000) map of your area to put on the wall, with map-pins and small labels indicating all the local sights. Maps can be obtained rolled, rather than folded. Some can be supplied plastic-coated to keep them clean; otherwise, cover the map with transparent plastic or 'Fend' so that it does not rapidly become fingermarked. I have seen an entire small wall covered with maps in this way, like wallpaper, and spotlit, which is decorative and interesting as well as useful. A lot of work to do, but once done it is permanent.

5 If you enjoy photography, consider amassing a lot of slides of local sights to project on (say) Saturday evenings for interested visitors to view; alternatively make (or buy from your regional Tourist Board, perhaps) a video-cassette to show. Cameras, etc., used for such purposes could be a tax-deductible expense.

6 Write out and photocopy itineraries for local car tours you can recommend, or footpath routes for walkers, if none have been published officially. Again, much work, but once done it need never be redone. It is worth including any recommendations you may have for pubs or other lunch places.

7 If you do not serve dinner, collect specimen menus from local restaurants, etc.

8 Before the season starts, telephone or call on some of the principal 'sights' in your vicinity and ask if they will give discounts on admission fees to visitors you send them. You will be surprised how many say yes, for their prices include a percentage for publicity expenditure, which they can discount.

9 Have accessible a list of local telephone numbers and addresses useful to your guests: doctor, dentist, chemist, railway station, coach or bus station, taxi rank, cycle and car hire, riding stables, boat trips, hairdresser, launderette, source of fishing permits, Tourist Information Centre, chiropodist, health club, vet, etc.

10 Stock up with local maps and guidebooks; rail and bus time-tables; theatre and other events lists; tide tables; details of sports facilities and spectator-sport events; fishing maps; information on local coach tours. Some Tourist Boards issue annual 'diaries' of events in their area.

11 Not only as a service but also as a source of profit, you could carry a small stock of books and maps for sale: a local book-shop might provide a stock.

12 At a Dorset house, an exercise book is prominently placed, with a label saying 'Comments on places visited by guests: please add yours'. This is a great success, and full of tips on places to visit and where to eat.

13 If you take out membership of a local sports club, your visitors may be able to sign in as your guests, free. (A tax-deductible expense.)

Extra services

In your less busy periods, you might like to offer visitors escorted walks, birdwatching or even car tours (for a fee); or it may be that there is someone else in the neighbourhood who would care to do this. Overseas visitors in particular seem to value such services. Offering to pick walkers up in your car at the end of a day's ramble is another idea.

Some hosts do a lot to involve selected visitors in local life, taking them along when they go to an auction, bell-ringing, a rugby match, the cattle market, a W.I. meeting or whatever. Some visitors are thrilled to be invited to things which are not part of the commercialised tourist circuit. This would not do for everybody, but when host and visitor find one another congenial company, this kind of thing is one of the extra rewards of getting into the bed and breakfast business. Feel your way carefully before starting to use first names: some visitors are not keen on this.

10.

Financial Matters

STARTING UP

If you are selling one house and moving to another, there will be not only the usual costs of house purchase (fees to lawyers and estate agents, removal, new furnishings) but also probably building alterations e.g. more lavatories, fees involved in getting various consents (see later), signboard, brochures, extra stocks of bedlinen (ideally three sets per bed) and tableware, extra beds and other furnishings, and possibly central heating. Many of these expenses may also arise if you are going to start offering bed and breakfast in your present home.

To get all this organised, and to allow for shopping around to find the best value, months of preparation time are needed before opening up to visitors at, say, Easter. During this time you will be paying out money (including your own living expenses) while nothing will be coming in, so allow for this.

At least when you do get going you have the advantage over some businesses in that customers pay for services received there and then, not a month later (indeed, through deposits they pay part in advance); and you do not have to order in stocks (of food, particularly) not knowing how long it will be before you resell it.

When buying at the outset such basic equipment as a cooker and washing-machine (or combined washer-dryer – an even greater labour saver), get the largest you can afford and accommodate. A large grill (for breakfasts) is particularly important. As bedroom carpets will need cleaning daily, a large (upright) vacuum cleaner, kept upstairs, is almost an essential to cover the area quickly, with another downstairs. There may be advantages to leasing equipment with a value of over £300; this saves capital outlay and is a tax-deductible expense.

When acquiring any major 'plant', give extra thought to any extended guarantee or maintenance contract that is offered, as it will get extra heavy use and you will be more dependent on it than an ordinary user (but watch for any exclusion clauses).

You may want a more sophisticated telephone than the standard instrument, such as a 'hands-free' one which you can use while your hands are writing down bookings, etc., or one with a built-in calculator, for example. Other more unusual appliances you may wish to consider are electric boot-dryers (especially if you intend to accommodate many walkers or anglers), electrically heated duvets, and electric firelighters for those open fires guests appreciate so much.

One of the heaviest expenses must be faced at the outset: really durable carpet for stairs and ground floor, which will get a lot of traffic. Top-quality carpet tiles (replaceable) may be a sensible choice in a hall. Carpets with small allover patterns can more readily be altered or patched should the need arise (and on stairs, avoid any design that obscures the edge of treads because your older visitors might misjudge them and stumble). Plentiful light (and light paint) can do much to uplift a house at minimum cost, leaving more expensive improvements for later.

In short, do not underestimate the extra capital expenditure you will incur sooner or later.

Raising money

There are various sources of grants or loans to help people start up. Borrowing from a bank should not be too difficult if the house can provide the security the bank will want before it will advance money, and if you can provide a well reasoned forecast of income, but should you fail to repay by the agreed date, it may claim the house. A loan may take the form of an overdraft – the cheapest form of borrowing there is – if all you need is to pay for equipment or wages to get going, before cash starts to come in. Interest rates can fluctuate during the period of a loan, but are never likely to be as dear a way to finance purchases as hire purchase is.

More substantial sums might be needed, however, for alterations or improvements to the house – amounts that may take years to repay. The bank manager will ask you to explain your plans, your reasons for supposing enough visitors will come to stay, and your estimates of future expenditure and income. He/she will judge your ability to carry out your plans. If you 'shop around' you may find one bank more helpful than another; rates of interest and other terms are negotiable, so there is no need to settle for whatever is first offered. If need be, a bank manager may be able to lend you money under the government's Loan Guarantee Scheme; and every bank has useful booklets for people starting their own small enterprises.

Think twice before seeking finance for extra bedrooms and their furnishings. These rooms will increase your overheads (interest on loans; more work of all kinds, perhaps more staff; more heat, rates, insurance; perhaps more advertising to fill them). I hear more complaints about making ends meet from people who have expanded than from those whose ventures are small.

Perhaps you are planning to run a bed and breakfast house because you have lost your job. In some circumstances, you might still be able to draw unemployment or supplementary benefit while doing so, if it is just a part-time activity and you do not make a lot out of it; but you must continue to register as 'available for work'. Much depends on the attitude of the local Social Security officials. You may be eligible for a free place at one of the useful training courses mentioned in a later chapter; or for an 'enterprise allowance' while you get going (ask about this at any Job Centre).

A useful source of finance and advice is the Rural Development Commission, 11 Cowley St., London SW1P 3NA – it also has county offices, if you intend to provide bed and breakfast in the countryside or a small town. This body is particularly concerned with enterprises in 'rural development areas' (regions which the government has designated as being in particular need of help; mainly in the north and north-east, on the Welsh borders, and in Devon and Cornwall) and particularly if your guest-house is going to provide some employment for local people, directly or indirectly. Apart from sometimes itself providing loans of up to 30% for purchase or improvement of property (not for equipping it), the commission has experts to help you prepare applications to banks, etc.; some who are specialists in the hotel, catering, and bed and breakfast field; others in marketing and publicity methods. Their management accountants can advise on getting your costing and pricing right, on obtaining grants from Tourist Boards, and on tax concessions. They may even prepare a feasibility study before you start, to determine whether your plans are well-founded or not. Banks are more willing to lend money if a project has Commission backing. In addition, there are technical advisers on things like building, getting planning permission, noise abatement, heating, and insulation. Advice is free in the first instance, with moderate fees thereafter.

Also, the Rural Development Commission may put you in touch with the skilled craftsmen you need to thatch the roof, build a wall or a built-in cupboard, make a wrought-iron gate, or re-upholster an antique chair; or they may tell you of two- to five-day courses to learn a skill such as upholstery yourself.

The Rural Development Commission grants will usually be for one quarter of the total cost. Improvements, extensions or repairs may also qualify for grant aid. The Rural Development Commission's free booklet *Old Buildings – New Opportunities* is full of useful information. The equivalents outside England are the Welsh Development Agency, Treforest Industrial Estate, Pontypridd, CF37 5UT (telephone 044 385 2666); the Scottish Development Agency, Rosebery House, Haymarket Terrace, Edinburgh, EH12 5EZ (telephone 031- 337 9595); and LEDU, Upper Galwally, Belfast, BT8 42B (telephone 0232 491031).

Other possible sources of grants include – depending on circumstances – the Ministry of Agriculture (for farmhouse bed and breakfast, particularly in upland areas, see later chapter); the regional Tourist Boards; English Heritage (if a house of exceptional historic interest is involved); the Department of Trade (in areas where industry has declined); the E.C. (their booklet, *Finance from Europe*, can be obtained from the London office, 8 Storeys Gate, London SW1P 3AT); your district council; for things like games-rooms or swimming pools, the Sports Council; and, for sporting projects (such as shooting-parties, or angling), the Game Conservancy or the Countryside Commission. The Rural Development Commission can advise on approaches to any of these (its free booklet *Action for Rural Enterprise* is a guide to the assistance available from a wide range of sources). Remember, too, the Job Release Scheme (financial help for older people who want to retire early), assistance which might be very useful in starting a bed and breakfast house.

Improving the house

For improvements or extensions to the house, a loan from a building society or bank may be obtainable, and it will qualify for tax relief. There is also tax relief in respect of loans for furnishings. No major alterations to a house, or change of its use (to a bed and breakfast business), should be done without your building society's agreement if you are still paying off your original mortgage. They may increase the interest rate slightly. Older people should enquire about interest-only mortgage payments – the repayment of the capital borrowed is not required until the house is sold or the borrower dies.

Grants from local councils (to improve pre-1962 houses, provide basic amenities, or to repair pre-1919 houses) are unlikely to be given in respect of a home that is being run as a bed and breakfast business, but if you want to pursue this possibility send for a free booklet, *Home Improvement Loans*, from the Halifax Building Society, Freepost, Halifax, HX1 2BR.

Citizens' Advice Bureaux are very knowledgeable about all these matters. Another source of guidance is the Small Firms Service of the Department of Industry, which has a number of regional offices at which up to three interviews are given free to anyone needing advice on business problems. (Simply dial 100, ask for Freefone 2444 and request leaflets with details.) Business in the Community (227a City Road, London EC1V 1LX) has a directory of 'enterprise agencies' throughout the country which give free counselling to anyone starting a business. This includes advice on finance, publicity, premises and training.

Special funds

Another avenue worth exploring may be the innumerable societies which exist to make loans or grants to help people from different walks of life (such as the armed services) who need assistance, or their widows or other dependants. Most libraries have the *Directory of Grant-making Trusts*, which lists these.

Grants and loans always take time to secure (much paperwork has to go to committees, as a rule), and grants may be taxable, and sometimes applications have to be accompanied by a fee, which is non-returnable. Take, for instance, the English Tourist Board's fund for guest-houses (available to existing ones making improvements as well as to new, but generally given only to projects of £5,000 or more). It may advance up to one-fifth of the total cost of providing such things as en suite bathrooms, central heating, ramps for wheelchairs, and swimming pools. Usually such grants (allotted on an annual first-come-first-served basis) go only to larger houses reaching a three crown standard – see chapter 6; and you must have any necessary planning permission already (that costs money, too), and an accountant's certificate for the intended expenditure. There are forms to fill in with estimates of what you will be spending and what you will be receiving (for years to come), and of what you will have to find for tax, interest on other loans, depreciation . . . the questions go on and on. You must not start work until the grant is agreed. For years, you will not be free to sell your property without permission, there will be inspections, and surveyor's certificates of work done (more fees) will be required.

So allow for the time and effort needed if you want financial help from any quarter.

Deciding on expenditure

Last but not least, is expenditure really necessary? How much extra trade will extra amenities bring in? Or, to pay for them, will you have to put up your charges so much that you risk pricing yourself out of your sector of the market?

In deciding what to provide for guests, why not, before going to great expense, find out what they want, by the rather obvious method of asking them? The owner of a farm in Warwickshire gave her guests a questionnaire to answer; as a result of this she learned that, yes, 96% would be prepared to pay £2 a night extra for en suite bathrooms; but, no, 79% did not want bedroom TVs. A similar exercise at another house revealed that expenditure on bedroom kettles and teacups would be worthwhile, as more guests preferred this to tea brought up on trays – which causes extra work.

RUNNING COSTS

Costs that can fluctuate with the number of guests are:

breakfast (and any other meals);
laundering bedlinen and towels;
bedroom heating and hot water;
casual wages;
(possibly, commission to be paid to booking agents or credit card companies).

It might be assumed that anything a guest paid for bed and breakfast would, after deducting the above, be profit or a return for your labour. But hidden costs come to far more – perhaps double; and many bills have to be paid regardless of whether you have many guests or none:

fuel for the house as a whole – make sure you are on the most economical gas and electricity tariffs;
your mortgage, interest on bank loan, etc.;
rates and water rate (unless water is metered);
insurances;
postage, stationery, printing, advertising;
telephone – do all the phoning you can on the cheap rate, after 6 p.m.; and do not make calls on behalf of guests without charging them;
downstairs cleaning;
servicing (boilers, etc.).

These are regular costs and are largely predictable, at least after your first year. Others that come infrequently (and sometimes unexpectedly, for which reason you need to accumulate reserves to meet them) include:

income tax, annually;

your accountant's fees, annually;

interior and exterior redecoration (if you accept smokers, rooms will have to be redecorated at least every three to four years);

major repairs (sometimes very unexpected – a new roof would cost thousands);

major renewals (mattresses, armchairs and kitchen appliances).

Even the regular costs may go up unexpectedly: rates (or the new community charge), heating and mortgage interest are three examples of costs that are subject to sudden and steep changes quite out of your control. At one place, within five years rates had gone up 120%, insurances 50%, and heating 200%.

Some people drift along with little idea of what even their most basic costs really are. Experienced hoteliers attending a refresher course were given a list of ingredients served for a typical breakfast and were asked to price these. Answers ranged between 50p and £2.50! (The correct answer was variously estimated a few years ago at 70p or 85p.) No wonder so many go out of business so frequently.

And how do you value your time? It has been estimated (by Exeter University) that running the simplest bed and breakfast house takes about 28 hours a week; an underestimate if you allow for time spent talking to guests, dealing with telephone and paperwork, and keeping up a high standard – brass gleaming, flowers fresh, curtains washed, and really good cooking. (One guest-house owner said that she and her husband work 16 hours a day, 7 days a week, for 10 months of the year.) It is not customary to add any service charge to bills, in the way that hotels do; and you will be unwise to pay yourself wages (which would be subject to PAYE tax). So you are working for whatever profits you can make and for the tax reliefs which, although they apply to running a business, help to cover your own food and accommodation.

114

Covering your costs

Your accountant will be able to help you estimate, on the basis of the above items, how many bed and breakfast visitors you need at a given price to cover these costs. Whether you will be able to secure that many bookings is a matter for your own judgment. You may have the records of the previous owner to guide you, or promises of bookings from some nearby college or firm, for instance. Be alert to competitors that might take bookings from you – not just other bed and breakfast houses but, for instance, a self-catering development nearby or a large and posh hotel that is starting to offer bargain breaks at very low prices. On average, most guest-houses achieve only 50% occupancy per annum (number of bed spaces multiplied by number of nights available = 100% occupancy; if only half of that total are actually let, this is 50% occupancy). In the first year of operation, that figure might be only 30%. On the other hand, you might be lucky and achieve above-average occupancy at the outset.

The table overleaf will give you an idea of how many bed-nights (left-hand column) you need to achieve to cover your costs. (A bed-night means one person for one night; thus a couple occupying a double room for two nights = four bed-nights.)

Setting your prices

Pricing is a tricky question. A newcomer's priority is to fill his or her rooms, even if at little profit, because repeats and recommendations – the most important part of future trade – depend on this, so it might seem to make sense to start off with moderate prices to attract plenty of visitors (though not so low that discriminating people think the house can be no good). But if this proves successful, you will be hard put to it to justify a sudden leap in your prices next year unless you have added extra amenities: people will not be pleased to be asked to pay more than the friends who recommended them, or far above the

	Average value of one bed-night (including any meals, drinks, etc.):				
No. of bed-nights sold in a year:	£10	£15	£20	£25	£30
100	1000	1500	2000	2500	3000
200	2000	3000	4000	5000	6000
300	3000	4500	6000	7500	9000
400	4000	6000	8000	10000	12000
500	5000	7500	10000	12500	15000
600	6000	9000	12000	15000	18000
700	7000	10500	14000	17500	21000
800	8000	12000	16000	20000	24000
900	9000	13500	18000	22500	27000
1000	10000	15000	20000	25000	30000

rates they have found in a year-old accommodation guide. From the outset, it is better to price your accommodation realistically, in relation to what you and your local competitors have to offer, than to risk such loss of goodwill.

Children's rates

Where you can be flexible is in children's rates, if yours is the sort of place for family holidays. Whereas a couple taking a short break are not likely to decide on one place rather than another for the sake of a pound or two a night, a parent will calculate the cost of a week's holiday with children quite carefully. Reductions for children (assuming that you want to attract them) may be crucial in securing business of this kind; as may reductions for week-long holidays (for which July and August are the peak months).

Some places have a simple half-rate tariff for children, which is expensive for three-year-olds (perhaps deliberately) but a bargain for older children, who can eat at least as much as adults. Others offer graduated tariffs, increasing at every few years of age. Large reductions may be given when children are sharing a family room, with only perhaps 10% off for children occupying a room of their own. It is important to be able to quote children's rates immediately and not vaguely to say it depends on how much they eat. On the other hand, it is wise not to apply any rule about shared rooms too strictly if you may lose a good booking by making the holiday too expensive. For babies, you may choose to make no charge, or a nominal one to cover the use of a cot and the hot water they require even if they consume no food.

Room for manoeuvre

Prices can be increased annually by a modest amount. Not only has inflation to be considered but also the unexpected – (e.g. a leap in fuel prices) that may take you unawares in mid-season. If you are approaching a VAT level of trade (see later), remember that you may have to start paying VAT in mid-season after your prices have been published; and if you fail to do so, the Customs & Excise will ultimately demand payment of these arrears (plus interest). Always allow in your prices for a proportion to be put aside against future repairs and redecorations: it is not a good idea to have (say) re-wiring done with the intention of bumping up next season's prices steeply to pay for it: why should next season's visitors be penalised for your failure to have budgeted ahead? Improved facilities (like en suite bathrooms) may reasonably command higher prices, provided you have a clientèle able to pay extra: if you have hitherto relied mainly on, say, young walkers or elderly people on a pension, they may not be able to afford more.

The common practice of raising prices at the beginning of each year is irrational, for it is hard enough to get visitors then without inflicting a price rise too. Winter is a time for discounts, if you are open to visitors, and spring for increases.

You can perhaps have the best of both worlds if you have some superior rooms with en suite bathrooms to let at high prices, and one or two more basic rooms at lower prices. This flexibility is useful for other reasons, too, making it easier to offer even the superior rooms at a lower price when trade is slack, which is far better than having them stand empty. A tour operator may want you to offer his or her clients rooms at a discount, which you might wish to do in order to fill empty beds. If this became known to other visitors paying full price for equivalent accommodation, they might feel irritated. However, having varied room rates makes deals of this sort easier.

Such deals can be very important in tourism because demand is so variable and unpredictable. Almost anything is better than an empty room. To accept a very late booking at a cut price is better than taking nothing. To offer free accommodation at slack periods (Sunday nights perhaps) can be worthwhile if this is conditional upon visitors staying a certain length of time and/or buying meals.

Assessing the market

People who use bed and breakfast accommodation are, almost by definition, price-conscious; and if your prices approach those of hotels, they may well decide that hotels are better value.

Covering your costs and making a profit is one way to arrive at the price to charge for bed and breakfast, but there are other considerations. Questions to ask yourself are these.

What prices do others in the area charge? (But how fully booked are they; and are their rooms of a higher or lower standard than yours?)

What kind of visitors come to your area? (Businessmen can usually afford to pay more than most tourists, tourists more than most students.)

Have you got to incorporate in your prices VAT, 10% commission to a booking agency or the 4% or so taken by credit card companies (the last two items will relate to only some bookings, but their cost must be spread over all)? Note that it is illegal to quote prices exclusive of VAT.

Are you going to include in your price things which at some houses are added to the bill as extras (morning tea is an

118

example)? Charging extra for baths or bedroom heating are dying practices. I have found one house where £1 extra is charged if a visitor wants to stay in the house all day long, expecting heat and tea to be provided. Charging small sums for such extras is altogether too reminiscent of the (mythical?) seaside landladies who used to charge for the use of the salt and pepper: it is better, if you wish to provide such services, to cost them into your basic price and give a hospitable impression rather than a grasping one.

Will you charge the same for every room, or more for one that has (for instance) a fourposter bed or sea view?

Will you offer any discounts on your prices? For example: a reduction to those who stay more than, say, three or seven nights; or who come for 'bargain breaks' in slack seasons? (If your winter prices are lowered, while your heating bills go up, and yet you still get few visitors then, it may be better to close down till spring.) Or to former visitors as an inducement to come again?

Conversely, will you put prices up at peak periods (summer, Christmas, Easter)? To give a discount at one season always gives a better impression than to impose a surcharge at another even if the result is the same: but at some houses there is a surcharge on July-August prices for stays of only a night or two because these may push out the week-long holidaymakers who, predominantly, come in those months – and for them normal rates are usually available.

The top of the market

Bed and breakfast can these days be a very upmarket affair, with as much as £30 being charged for one night's bed and breakfast, £15 for dinner – more, much more, in a lordly castle with butler. But for prices like that something very special indeed has to be provided; and probably many visitors will be Americans able to pay for an experience of British country house hospitality at its most luxurious. There are a number of agencies through whom such visitors can be obtained – at a price (see chapter 7). Other people are more likely to argue that for money like this they could have a trip to the Mediterranean. And remember it is now possible to stay at quite high-ranking hotels, on their bargain-break terms, for £40 – £60 (two days' half board) and children free, on any days of the year – in en suite rooms with TV and all the trimmings. They give these discounts on their normal high prices (as paid by business-men, for the most part) in order to fill rooms that would other-wise be empty. Two things can be learnt from this. One is that if your prices get near to these prices, some prospective visitors will opt for a hotel. The other is that if you offer two-day bargain breaks, at least at slack seasons, you may get more trade.

However, perfectionists will always want to keep on im-proving even at the risk of pricing themselves beyond the reach of many visitors. One proprietor, when asked why his prices had gone up from £16 (half board) to £24 in six years, gave several reasons: (1) giving every bedroom a colour television, hair-dryer, telephone, teamaker and heated towel rail – the running costs of which (over and above the capital outlay) came to £1 a room; (2) providing 13 choices at breakfast and an à la carte choice at dinner, the preparation of which takes six hours; (3) fully equipping a laundry room, used by guests; (4) annual redecoration throughout; (5) upgrading furniture, china, etc.

Maximising your income

Some people who find they are not making enough out of their bed and breakfast business think the answer is to increase prices. But a few, having done so, have had to reduce them again. It is better to think of ways to fill beds at present empty, or to make more money per guest by other means – a drinks licence (some hotels make more money on drinks than on food)? selling soft drinks? selling antiques, home-made chocolates and preserves or crafts? selling plants (a greenhouse might be a good investment)? incentives to stay another night or two? Perhaps your mix of single/double/twin/family rooms is not right – what kind of enquiries are you not at present satisfying? Always strive first to fill any beds that are empty in peak seasons; filling them in other seasons takes second place.

Here are some of the initiatives used at various houses:

refrigerator with help-yourself drinks and snacks, priced (visitors write in a book what they have taken);

free Sunday lunch (or free wine) or free Sunday night – nearly always a bad night for bookings – to those staying for a minimum of three days (Thursday to Saturday nights);

'sampler breaks' in spring with option to book, before leaving, a full summer holiday at a discount;

children accommodated free if a full week is booked;

mid-week bargain breaks for over-60s (if mid-week bookings are fewer than weekend ones);

wives accommodated free at weekends if husband (staying mid-week on business) stays on for two more days;

discount vouchers for admission to tourist attractions, etc., for visitors staying at least a week.

One of the best things to achieve is a repeat visit from a satisfied guest (for one thing, there is no advertising cost involved in securing this business), or from a friend to whom he has recommended you. This can be achieved mainly by ensuring that the guest has a good time on the first occasion, but also by reminding him at the right moment (see chapter 9) or offering a discount. If he has had any disappointing experience, consider making a reduction on the bill – for example, in respect of building work in progress or a plumbing failure.

Prolonging the season

Securing more bookings outside high summer is not as hard as it used to be. In most areas, the tourist season now spreads into spring and autumn – even winter in places like Bath and Canterbury where there is plenty to do all round the year – but mainly for short breaks. To encourage this, a small hotel in Cumbria provides a month by month weather chart of the last six years to show that the climate outside summer need not deter. Chapter 11 describes 'activity' breaks which attract visitors in winter. Other inducements may be financial, such as the offer of two free nights out of four, on condition that four dinners are bought (at a place where dinners are carefully costed to make a profit).

Small bed and breakfast houses, being more flexible than big hotels, can try out all sorts of ideas like this, provided a little imagination is brought to bear on the problem.

The value of records

Finding out, in your first year, who your visitors are and why they have come will help you plan your publicity strategy for next year. Keep a record card for each (useful if they come back), with notes like 'elderly couple, like quiet, don't eat fish' or 'businessman, uses phone a lot'. At the end of the season, you can analyse these records to good effect. And *always* ask 'How did you hear of us?' and jot the answer down: from this you will find out what results you are getting from your advertising, and whether repeats and recommendations are running high – if not, something is wrong with your standards. Each card should show how long the visitor stayed and what he spent (someone taking bed and breakfast only for three days could be of less value than a one-nighter taking dinner and paying for extras such as drinks: what can you do to attract more of the latter?); or instead of record cards you could use the back of the carbon copy of their bill for notes.

Studying how long people stay, on average, might be revealing too. Suppose two nights was the average. You might next season offer discounts for three-night stays, and then see whether this converted many two-nighters to three. If not, your discount is money thrown away and you will know better the year after that.

You could pick from your record cards spring and summer visitors to whom it might be worthwhile sending a special offer of an autumn break.

In short, raising prices to increase income should be a last, not a first, resort.

One-night visitors

A major problem for most bed and breakfast houses is the mobility of today's tourists and their tendency to make one-night stops. To have a succession of these means constant bed-linen changes, daily bills, and little personal contact: altogether unprofitable. The situation is even worse if you have accepted a one-nighter and therefore had to turn away a subsequent request for several nights, and then the one-nighter cancels or does not turn up. Some bed and breakfast proprietors combat this nuisance by such means as the following.

Accept one-nighters only if the booking is made that day, and the room would otherwise be empty.

Refuse one-nighters in high season, or at peak periods like weekends, Easter, etc., or if they do not intend to take dinner too. Conversely, you may accept them at short notice for bed and breakfast only, so that no food is wasted if they don't turn up.

Impose a £2 surcharge on one-night bookings or (better) offer a £2 discount for longer stays (the actual prices being the same).

Require payment in advance (in case of cancellation).

However, many people report that people who come for one night often stay longer, or return another time for a proper stay, after they have found the place enjoyable. At a farm in Oxfordshire an American who stayed one night sent – over the years – nine others, who each stayed longer; another farm has a regular visitor who first came for one night and has since been back five times with husband, child and friends.

Profit from food and wine

Prices for evening meals are another problem area. Restaurants usually take the cost of the food and roughly treble it to arrive at a price that allows for overheads, labour and a 10% profit. They are operating on a much larger scale, of course, and have costs that a bed and breakfast house does not. Even so, many bed and breakfast proprietors tell us that it is impossible to make money on a meal priced at £8 or so if there are very few guests to cater for (the labour involved is almost as great for few as for many diners, and there are no economies of scale to be made in buying foodstuffs). If there is a nearby inn or bistro offering good but cheap meals, they simply cannot compete on price. Nevertheless, there may be visitors prepared to pay a bit more for the convenience and pleasure of dining at your house, enjoying freshly prepared home food (even if only a simple omelette and salad), rather than go out: it entirely depends what type of visitor you get, how far you are from other eating-places and your own inclination for shopping and cooking.

One way in which many bed and breakfast houses have an advantage over restaurants is wine. Some visitors like the economy (and choice) of bringing their own. And if you do have a drink licence, you will certainly be able to compete on price, by not imposing the hefty mark-up on wine which most restaurants do.

Taking bookings

Here are some tips about taking bookings, by phone or letter.

1 Record them in a very large desk diary, with a column drawn for each room; and use pencil not pen, because changes quite often occur.
2 Ensure the visitor knows the price inclusive of any VAT or service charge and any extras.
3 Check that when he says 'from the 25th to the 29th' that he does not mean he will be leaving on the morning of the 29th (i.e. four nights not five).
4 At what time will he arrive, and will he then need a meal (if you provide this)?
5 Check that he knows how to find your house.
6 Write down his requirements as to: double or twin beds? en suite bathroom (if available) or not? Any particular foods he does not eat?
7 If he asks for a particular bedroom, say you will do your best but don't guarantee it (if you do, you may find you have no room for manoeuvre when another visitor wants it, for a longer period).

8 Ask for a deposit (you can name whatever amount you choose
but one-third for a short stay and one-quarter for a long one
are reasonable sums), and written confirmation with
estimated time of arrival (saying you will keep the room for
up to an hour after that). Some houses insist that if there is no
deposit, because a booking has been made too late to send
this, the visitor must turn up by 4 p.m. (For an alternative,
see credit cards below.)

9 Sometimes a caller will book in during the afternoon, saying
he will return later. In this case, ask him to leave his baggage
in the bedroom. Such callers (and some who book by phone)
go from one house to another reserving rooms for the night,
turning up only at the one they favour most.

Some women running bed and breakfast houses on their own
think it a wise precaution not to let rooms to single men (unless
referred by a local business company) nor to open the door after
6 p.m. (unless a visitor is expected).

Bookings, incidentally, are increasingly made at short notice.
The days are gone when most people booked in January for
their summer holidays in Britain. And finally, if family or staff
take phone calls, it is essential that they understand how
important telephone manners are.

Payment

Tor Haven (Devon) finds it eliminates misunderstandings to
give visitors the form on the next page soon after their arrival,
the upper part having been completed at the time of booking
and the 'additional purchases' part waiting to be completed on
their departure.

As indicated on the form, cheque cards are of use only for
sums under £50 (when writing its number on the back of a
cheque, check its expiry date); but a visitor could pay his bill in
instalments, each £50 of it being paid on different days (it is not
wise to accept several £50 cheques from the same person on the
same date: this may invalidate the guarantee of payment).

If you have a credit card account, you can use it for taking
deposits – handy when a booking is made by telephone too late

---

Mr/Mrs   Date:

With Compliments

This account - due for settlement on the morning of departure - is presented for your convenience. Cheques up to £50 are accepted with a cheque card. Cheques above £50 must be submitted at least four working days (not weekends) prior to departure. Multiple cheques issued on the same day are not covered by a cheque card.

A supplementary account will be provided for any additional purchases made during your stay. Thank you.

No. of Guests	No. of Nights	Nightly Rate			
		£	(B&B/DB&B)	£	
		£	(B&B/DB&B)	£	
			Total	£	
			Less Deposit	£	
			Accommodation Total	£	

Additional Purchases

Bar   Restaurant

£

Amount Due £

Less Paid on Account £

S	M	T	W	T	F	S
DBB/BB	DBB/BB	DBB/BB	DBB/BB	DBB/BB	DBB/BB	DBB/BB

TOTAL DUE: £

Inclusive of V.A.T. 15%

Service Charge is not included: Gratuities are left to your discretion.

Room	Received on:	The sum of:

for a deposit to be posted (the visitor need only quote his number on the telephone). If a visitor then fails to turn up, you are liable to compensation (if the room remains unlet), and you can again charge his credit card account.

If you do accept a cheque without a cheque card and it

'bounces', or if you have any other claim against a visitor (for damage done, for not turning up, etc.), you can use the Small Claims Court procedure. This is how a Wiltshire bed and breakfast proprietor set about recovering £120. 'After paying a £12 fee, I filled in the details of my claim on a form. The man who had given me the dud cheque was informed by the court that I was making a claim. When after three weeks he had still not paid up, I asked the court to proceed further and they served a summons on him, fixing a date for the matter to be heard. As so often happens, this did the trick and he sent the £120 plus the £12 fee (I might have claimed for my time too, but I didn't bother)'.

However, she was lucky: if the defendant contests a claim, the case will be heard in his local court, not yours, and you will be at a disadvantage if you do not put in an appearance. This may be more trouble than it is worth, but the procedure is at least a useful bluff. It costs little if you do not win, unless the defendant enters a counter-claim against you for any reason.

If you accept any cheque other than sterling (a traveller's cheque, for instance, or anything in foreign currency), your bank will make quite a substantial charge for accepting it: find out about this early in the season if you want to add a surcharge to bills paid this way.

Cancellation insurance

For a tourist to take out an insurance policy is normal when booking a holiday abroad, but the practice has not caught on for holidays in this country. This is probably because the really alarming risks, such as foreign medical expenses and un-scheduled return flights, will not occur.

Nevertheless, it is possible for British holidaymakers to insure against enforced cancellation, the consequent loss of their deposit, and their liability to their hosts. The usual grounds for a claim include illness or injury or that of a close relative, business associate or travelling companion; jury service; and redundancy. Some policies also cover other risks such as personal accident and loss of luggage or money while on holiday, and provide for additional travelling expenses resulting from accident or illness.

You can, if you wish, offer your visitors such insurance when they book, doing so either for the sake of the small commission you will get from the insurance company you deal with or, if you offer it free, as an inducement to visitors to book with you rather than elsewhere – whether this would be effective, it is impossible to judge.

If insurance is optional, few people are likely to take it up, and you may not find the paperwork involved is worth the small return. If you offer it free to all visitors who book for, say, more than three days, which you might consider as an alternative to offering a discount on your basic price, then the volume of business will be greater and therefore of more interest to an insurance company. A small hotel on the south coast has found it worthwhile to offer free cancellation insurance to visitors who book their next year's holiday before they leave. You can, of course, be your own insurer as far as cancellations are concerned. That is, ask visitors to pay £2.50 with their reservation (in addition to the deposit) as insurance against having to cancel and compensate the proprietor.

Some organisations make cancellation insurance compulsory, requiring clients to add the premium to the deposit they send. But this is hard to justify, and such a high-handed demand might put visitors off if a small guest-house tried to impose it.

If you wish to take the idea of cancellation insurance further, it would be best to approach the local office of one of the few well known companies that handle such business, or an insurance broker specialising in the travel trade. Your regional Tourist Board may have a scheme for its members, or you could discuss the matter with your own insurance broker when arranging the other special insurances you will undoubtedly be taking out.

If your object is to protect your own interests against 'no-shows' (people who book but do not turn up) your best insurance policy is probably to set your deposit at a realistically high level. This will discourage people from booking if they have any doubt that they will take up the reservation, and it will help to offset the money you lose by a no-show. (While the legal liability of a no-show will usually be greater than this deposit, recovering the difference, unless it is very large, is often more trouble than it is worth, even through the Small Claims Court.) One small consolation: VAT is not payable for sums taken in compensation from no-shows.

ACCOUNTS AND TAXES

However small your operation, it is worth getting a good accountant because he or she is likely to know so many ways of reducing your income tax liability. Some accountants advertise in their local paper or the Yellow Pages. Lists of qualified ones can be obtained from the Institute of Chartered Accountants (Moorgate Place, London, EC2P 2BJ). Or ask your bank manager or solicitor.

An accountant can also advise you on things like partnerships, raising finance, forecasting profits, selecting a pension scheme, insurances, and whether your income tax coding is likely to change (for better or worse).

Here are other ways in which an accountant's services could be invaluable.

1 Picking a date from which to start your first set of accounts (to avoid including more peak-period revenue than is essential); and a date on which to stop trading, if that arises, to minimise the hefty capital gains tax you will incur if you later sell a house where a bed and breakfast business has been run.
2 Obtaining tax relief for the depreciation of furnishings, kitchen appliances, typewriter, sewing machine and much else (about one quarter of their value, per annum).
3 Offsetting any loss you make in one year against the profits in others (before or after). When starting up you might make a loss for several years: an accountant can tell you how this might be offset against your income for the previous three years, which means the tax collector should repay some of the tax you had paid in those years.
4 Obtaining tax relief on supplies such as food; advertising; heating; cleaning, rates and phone; repairs and replacements; postage and stationery; magazines and membership

subscriptions; accountancy and legal costs; bank charges and interest on loans; insurances; staff; car if partly used in the course of your work.

5 Spreading the uneven incidence of major bills like gas, electricity and phone (which come quarterly); rates and income tax (twice yearly); insurances (annually).

Tax relief can be so substantial as to be a major reason why some people choose to run their home as a bed and breakfast house, even though they make little obvious profit. The effect of claiming tax relief on things like your rates, heating, food, insurance and much else could be to reduce your cost of living very substantially, but a sum in respect of 'personal use' has to be agreed with your tax inspector and is then excluded from tax relief. Some inspectors are tougher than others when it comes to deciding what the sum should be.

At the same time, you may be able to raise your standard of living if extra amenities can be charged as an expense of the business. I have in mind such things for the house or garden as conservatory, summerhouse, barbecue, patio, swimming pool, tennis court, double glazing, kitchen improvements, sauna, improved bathrooms, video recorder, exercise bicycle, sunbed, snooker, table tennis, piano, boat, beach hut, garden seating or anything else which you can legitimately claim is for your guests' use.

Just like any business, you need to keep a proper record of payments and receipts for tax purposes: an accountant will set up a simple system for you, and do your tax return every year – ensuring you get every allowance or relief to which you are entitled, which will make his fee an economy in the long run.

Value added tax

Should your annual gross receipts exceed a certain five-figure sum (which goes up annually), you are obliged to register for VAT and add VAT (currently 15%) to everything you charge your visitors, passing this on to Customs and Excise every quarter. However, you can reclaim from Customs and Excise all the VAT you have had to pay out on supplies – more paperwork! This may not amount to much, however, if your biggest expenditure is on food (which carries no VAT, though cleaning materials, confectionery and other household items do). It is important to be alert to the risk that, as your business grows, you may enter the VAT bracket in mid-season, when you cannot raise prices already advertised (which is why some people quote their price 'plus VAT', in case this happens; but this is rather offputting to visitors). Should you fail to hand over VAT as soon as you become liable, Customs and Excise will make a back-dated claim for it when they find out, irrespective of whether you have collected it from your visitors or not. A particularly tiresome feature of VAT is that Customs and Excise look at your figures quarterly: you might enter the VAT bracket in a summer quarter, then fall below it in winter. And another hazard is that if any person (or their spouse) runs another business too, both will be added together and, if their combined total is at the VAT level, each will then have to carry VAT. I know of one house that is deliberately closed for one month each year to avoid falling into the VAT trap and the consequent price increases which may discourage visitors.

Book-keeping

Unless your bookings are very few, it may be worth employing a local book-keeper to come in perhaps once a month to write up your account books for you. Keeping proper accounts will save your accountant a lot of time (remember he or she charges by the hour, and professional services are never cheap) when he or she comes to do your annual income tax return. Alternatively take a short course in basic book-keeping. But, whether you or a book-keeper writes up the accounts, you will need to keep in good order the papers from which these figures are taken: cheque stubs, bank paying-in book (do not use loose paying-in slips), bank statements, bills and receipts for goods you have bought, carbon copies of bills you hand to visitors. Obviously, your bed and breakfast finances should be in a separate bank account from your personal one.

Your accountant will advise on what sort of account books the figures should be recorded in, but he or she is likely to recommend three sets of figures.

First, an account book in which to write down every bill you pay (with VAT in a separate column), under such headings as:

> Food and drink (including your family's);
> Gas, electricity, coal, oil;
> Rates, water rates;
> Phone;
> Car running expenses;
> Repairs, improvements;
> Stationery, printing, postage;
> Insurances;
> Rentals (TV, etc.);
> Bank charges, mortgage repayments;
> Household renewals;
> Servicing (e.g. of fire fighting appliances and boiler);
> Garden supplies.

In a separate book, a record of items paid for with cash – which might be milk, newspapers, domestic help, gardener, window cleaner, purchases at local shops. This is best done daily, as memory is fallible. But the more of these you can get on monthly credit accounts the better, especially such things as milk and petrol.

Thirdly, a record of income from guests, in a book with columns for accommodation, meals, drinks and any extras (with VAT, if any, shown separately). The simplest way is to give guests bills itemised in this manner, with a carbon copy for yourself: essential documentation for you (or your accountant) to satisfy the tax inspector and VAT man.

Possibly one to two hours a week is needed for all this, even in a small establishment, but the work is as vital as cooking breakfasts. Totalling everything up monthly will tell you how you are doing; quarterly totals are necessary for VAT purposes; and annual totals for your tax return.

Other financial matters

Here are some other financial considerations to bear in mind, all of them matters on which an accountant can give good advice.

Allow, if necessary, for paying all your own national insurance contributions as a self-employed person (see below).

As a 'sole trader', not a limited company, you will incur unlimited liability for any debts you run up; and, for the sake of your dependants, you need to think what financial provision is needed against the risk of illness or death preventing your carrying on.

For tax reasons, it may be better in a husband-wife (or other) partnership for one to be the employee of the other. If friends enter into a partnership which does not work out well, disentangling the matter can be exceedingly difficult and bitter. A solicitor should draw up a formal deed of partnership early on, defining the role and financial commitment of each, the shares of profits (or losses), whether one partner has overall contol or not, provision for altering the partnership and arbitration in disagreements, arrangements for banking and for audited accounts, and provision in the event of sickness or death of one partner. If one partner defaults on income tax, the other will have to pay the lot.

The tax inspector needs to be notified that a business has been established: the Inland Revenue's booklet *Starting in Business* explains everything to do with tax. Another booklet to get (from Customs and Excise) is *Should I be registered for VAT?*.

Self-employed people may be able to avoid the expense of making Class 2 national insurance contributions if their earnings are small. On the other hand, you may additionally have to make a Class 4 contribution based on your profits. And the situation is even more complex if you combine bed and breakfast with some other job, are a wife sheltering under her husband's contributions, and so on. Your accountant or the local DHSS office should advise; the latter provides relevant leaflets.

INSURANCE

In a purely domestic situation, most householders find an ordinary policy (covering the house and its contents against theft, fire and other such hazards) is sufficient. But such a policy does not cover a house where paying guests are taken.

Insurance may be a heavy expense, so it pays to shop around or, better still, to use a reputable insurance broker – *not* an insurance agent – to do so for you (list obtainable from British Insurance Brokers' Association, 14 Bevis Marks, London EC3 7NT; telephone: 01-623-9043). You should get a lower premium if you close in winter.

You may be wise to have public liability insurance in case a guest (or employee) is injured on your premises or his or her property is damaged; and what about insurance against hazards that might put your house out of action for months – a fire, breakdown of central heating, your own illness or accident? Insuring employees (even part-time cleaners) is compulsory by law. Good brokers should advise on what you do not need as well as what you do, and whether to go for an all-embracing package, described below, or separate policies. You do not have to pay them (they get commission from insurance companies) and they can be sued if they give wrong advice.

Only insurance can cover you against the damage which visitors occasionally do through sheer stupidity like putting hot haircurlers on a plastic surface or a travel iron on a carpet. You can hardly (though one hotelier did) charge a guest £25 for a replacement after a toilet-seat cracked when she sat on it.

Within one season, a Somerset guest-house had these experiences. A visitor let the shower curtain hang outside the bath instead of in: result, a flooded floor, the ceiling below came down, and that bedroom was therefore unlettable for days. Another shaded a lamp with a towel, which caught fire and destroyed the lamp. A third blocked a toilet with a disposable nappy. Another left an indelible stain on the bedroom carpet. Such a catalogue of trouble is rare indeed; and transgressors can be asked to pay or prosecuted through the Small Claims Court (see above). But sometimes damage, like a blocked toilet, is discovered only after a visitor has gone – perhaps back to another country. When visitors do offer to pay before departing, it is difficult to assess the likely cost of repair or replacement on the spot. Insurance may be the only answer (and even then you may have to stand part of the cost yourself, depending on your policy).

Be alert to what any insurance policy actually covers – in particular, loss of profits. You may get back the cost of repair or replacement after a disaster, but this may be a smaller sum than the income you have lost while a room is out of use, and your policy may not cover this. Note too that, if a significant claim is being made, the insurance company may not even let you start repairs until they have sent an assessor or loss adjustor to estimate the cost.

There are special guest-house policies which offer a comprehensive package for any place that takes visitors. Such a policy covers public liability (including food poisoning); damage to 'stock' (that can mean cigarette burns on furniture, for example, and maybe the breakdown of a freezer full of food); theft of contents – your goods or your guests' – (possibly with money and silver included, but not always); loss of business after (for instance) a fire – but not necessarily loss of business for some other reason (failure of the central heating system, for example). It is not likely to cover breakages (and replacing china with matching pieces can be an expensive business), nor any loss of your own personal property (see Appendix).

It is possible to be over-anxious (and to over-insure). Although some people say they have to replace 20 or 30 coat-hangers every year (and even otherwise honest people seem to think books are fair game), on the other hand, at one house which is full of antiques and small treasures like snuff boxes I was told that, far from losing anything, they have gained – an assortment of towels, slippers and so forth left behind! (This is a common experience – and, alas, when property is posted back to owners, postage is rarely refunded.) Some people deliberately under-describe their valuable antiques when writing their brochures, for fear of inviting burglary.

The other kind of insurance which you may, when self-employed, wish to take out is personal. Being your own boss means an irregular income, providing your own pension and sickpay, no entitlement to unemployment benefit, and having to take sole responsibility for the viability of the enterprise. It is possible to insure against the risk of being incapacitated for a long period (or even permanently); and there are also numerous pension plans for the self-employed. Your accountant can help you choose the best for your personal needs; or write to the Society of Pension Consultants (Ludgate House, London EC4 2AR).

LEGAL MATTERS

Running a bed and breakfast house does not involve you in such a web of laws as hotels and inns have to contend with: nearly thirty of them. For instance, you are not obliged to accommodate all comers and you are not liable for visitors' luggage (unless you are grossly negligent). Even if a bed and breakfast house describes itself rather grandly as the Laurels Hotel, it is still not a hotel in law unless it offers food, drink or a bed to 'any traveller' presenting himself.

However, there are a few points which it is important to observe, and more have been referred to in previous chapters.

1 Although business names (such as Greenways Guest House) do not have to be registered, it is a necessity if trading under such a name to put your own name too on business stationery. The business name has to be displayed on the premises.

2 If you misdescribe your premises, services or prices charged you can be prosecuted under the Trade Descriptions Act. (For instance, 'sea view' does not mean a glimpse of the waves from one corner of one balcony and a 'lounge' is not a combined sitting/dining-room: people have been heavily fined for these misdescriptions.)

3 In houses with four bedrooms or more, all prices, per night, should be displayed or handed over at the reception desk or entrance hall, before people book in.

4 When informing someone that a room is available for him, ask for his confirmation by a specified date, saying you will not keep the room thereafter. His acceptance, even orally, creates a legal contract obliging you to keep the room for him; but a written contract is better than an oral one.

5 If a guest cancels, you are required by law to attempt to relet his room; and may bill him (perhaps less an allowance for food not consumed, etc.) only after the relevant date has passed and the room has remained unlet. (In this context whenever you have to turn an enquirer away, keep his phone number with a view to calling him if a cancellation occurs.)

6 Provided checking-out time is displayed, a visitor who fails to vacate his room by then can be billed for an extra amount.

In some areas, there are solicitors with specialised knowledge of the hotel or bed and breakfast world. In fact, there are solicitors who themselves run bed and breakfast or guest-houses and therefore can advise from practical as well as theoretical experience. (see Appendix)

A solicitor's advice is virtually essential for house purchase, major planning issues, serious disputes with guests or suppliers (but see earlier description of the Small Claims Court procedure, for which a solicitor is not essential), and often when applying for the various licences and permits which are required for some activities.

You are more likely to succeed in a planning application for change of use (from a purely domestic dwelling to a bed and breakfast house) if you know what arguments carry most weight locally; and a local solicitor familiar with the local planning people can be a great help here. (For example, permission may be needed only if a majority of the bedrooms in your house are to be used for letting.) He or she probably has useful contacts on the parish council and similar bodies too.

A solicitor may help you to fight battles over such things as the rateable value of your house – a revaluation of non-domestic properties is to take place soon; or even such unexpected bolts from the blue as finding you are billed more for water or for refuse disposal on the grounds that you have become a commercial not just domestic user. Remember, there is no need to accept without argument a planning rejection, a rating valuation or any other official decision that goes against you. You are entitled to appeal, or to enlist the aid of your local councillor (even your local MP).

Many things previously taken for granted can suddenly attract official disapproval when you start doing bed and breakfast. (One example – having a pony or even a donkey around is subject to regulations when the public is present, even if it is not for guests to ride.) Fire regulations and drinks licences have been referred to in earlier chapters. Nearly every permission or licence application involves paying a fee to the authority concerned and, with a solicitor's fee on top of this, can be a costly exercise – particularly if an application is turned down.

If you operate without necessary planning or other permission and a local hotel, etc. sees you as serious competition, you may be denounced to the authorities.

Architects

Another type of professional you may need is an architect, particularly if making alterations to an historic building. The Society for the Protection of Ancient Buildings keeps a list of architects particularly experienced in this field (its address is 55 Great Ormond Street, London WC1 3JA). It could be useful to have a feasibility study done before you get too involved (See Appendix). A talk with a local architect who knows your area is always a good first step: the Client's Advisory Bureau of the Royal Institute of British Architects (66 Portland Place, London W1N 4AD; telephone 01-550-5533) can supply names.

Useful booklets

Free booklets worth sending for, as all contain useful financial or legal tips for small enterprises:

Starting your own business, and others	Small Firms Service
Employing People	(dial 100 and ask for
Should I be registered for VAT?	Freefone Enterprise).
Cashflow, and others	Dun and Bradstreet,
	26 Clifton Street, London EC2.
Action for Jobs: helping you to help yourself	From Job Centres. About enterprise allowances, loan guarantees, help for disabled workers etc.
Starting in Business	Any local tax office.
Loan Guarantee Scheme	Department of Employment, Tothill St, London SW1.

Guide for Self Employed	DHSS. Box 21, Stanmore,
Small Earnings from Self Employment	Middlesex, HA7 1AY.
Directory of Grants for Historic Buildings	Historic Buildings Commission,
	23 Savile Row, London WiX 2HE

Your local library or bookshop will have many books with titles like *Working from Home, Earning Money at Home, Working for Yourself, Money Guide for Women* and *Creating your own Work* from which you can pick up more useful tips and ideas.

The Small Business Guide (published by the BBC) is a glorified address book, and an invaluable one. On other pages are described some sources of finance or supplies, of expert advice or of training: this book lists hundreds. It also has a particularly helpful chapter on presenting your case when trying to raise money from a bank or other source. Highly recommended. *How to Buy a Business* (published by Kogan Page) discusses how and when to buy, and judging the worth of what you are buying. *A Woman's Guide to Starting her own Business* (Grafton paperback) is very down-to-earth and sensible – recommended for men too! Another worth buying is *Starting Your Own Business* (Consumers' Association). Among much other practical advice, it has a very good chapter on book-keeping and on the tricky matter of dismissing an employee. *Running Your Own Business* is free, from the Small Firms Division of the Department of Employment, Tothill Street, London SW1H 9NF, and worth getting for its three-page checklist of all the items you should have thought about before starting.

Useful free leaflets from tax inspectors' offices include: *Capital Gains Tax and the Small Business, CGT and Owner-Occupied Houses, Tax-Employed or Self Employed, PAYE* and *Thinking of Taking Someone On* (for employees), *Personal Allowances, Starting in Business, Bank Interest Tax, Thinking of Working for Yourself, Business Expansion Scheme.*

Additional income

What if, after all, the enterprise does not pay as well as you had hoped?

Bed and breakfast earnings usually fluctuate a lot, and some people with no other source of income will need to supplement them – possibly with winter work, and usually with work that can be done at home. A useful source of ideas is *Earning Money at Home* (a Consumers' Association book) which gives general advice and then covers such options as: cooking, or the sale of pastries and preserves, dressmaking and knitting, photography, repair work (from china to clocks and bicycles), book-binding, picture-framing, upholstery, indexing, crafts in great variety (e.g. soft toys), data preparation for market research, hiring things out, dealing by mail order in collectors' items including books, boarding or breeding animals, beekeeping, looking after children and using skills from a previous career (e.g. book-keeping, computers, teaching and coaching, electronics, secretarial, languages, hairdressing, etc.).

Other appropriate activities I have come across include 'granny-care' (in winter), secondhand dress or babywear agency, telephone-answering service, making Christmas cakes, agencies for various services (e.g. typing), consultancy or advisory work, outside catering for parties, and using one room for an antiques or art gallery.

Ceasing to trade

If for any reason you decide to give up doing bed and breakfast, plan ahead for the winding-down process. You may have to cancel visitors, advertisements and supplies; dismiss staff; inform bank, tax inspector and insurance companies; get your rates reduced; sell surplus equipment (via the local paper, *Exchange & Mart*, etc.). If you are selling your house as a bed and breakfast business, the buyer will, however, probably want you to keep everything up until he or she takes over. Give him or her all relevant records – bookings, deposits, useful addresses, your visitors' book and details of where you have been advertising.

Non-paying visitors

Finally, friends who learn you are starting a bed and breakfast house will want to come and stay, and you may then feel embarrassed to charge them, even though the accommodation they occupy is your livelihood. The solution is to forestall their proposal by inviting them – but for a winter visit, when you will have rooms empty. Alternatively, you can write accepting them at the season they want – and enclose your tariff.

11.
Sources of Supply, Advice and Information

Even before you begin (perhaps, *particularly* before you begin), you need a very large address book in which to accumulate useful information about where to obtain everything, from information and knowledge to everyday supplies. Other chapters of this book have already given a number of useful addresses that may be worth recording, and more follow. Don't forget other information sources already at your elbow – the Yellow Pages of the telephone directory and Thomson local directories – as well as your nearest Tourist Information Centre, Chamber of Commerce and Citizens' Advice Bureau; and you may get many useful contacts through joining your local tourism or guest-house association or simply by chatting to locals in your pub – an excellent way to get the names of dependable plumbers and electricians, for instance.

ADVICE AND HELP

Your regional Tourist Board may be able to distribute your brochure to Tourist Information Centres within a given radius of your house, or can give you a list so that you can do this yourself. It can advise you about your brochure and about advertising media in your region (but may know little more than anybody else how effective such advertising will prove) and offer you chances to be included in leaflets or directories they produce, usually for a charge. If you have something special that distinguishes you from every other bed and breakfast house, the board's press officer may be able to get you free editorial publicity in magazines or newspapers (see chapter 7). Expert advice on running a bed and breakfast house may be obtainable, and the board may organise workshops where you can swap notes with others in the business. Services like these are available, however, only to those who become members of the board, paying an annual subscription: what is available and what is charged differs from board to board. Addresses of all of them are in the appendix. The addresses of the Scottish, Welsh and Northern Ireland boards are in chapter 6.

The English Tourist Board has, among a large number of free and priced publications, a series of 8 development guides which offer advice and points of reference for the small businessman who is setting up a tourism enterprise. *Starting a small guest-house or bed and breakfast business*, produced in 1984, brings a number of points into consideration including legal and planning restraints. (Price £3 from Department D, Bromells Road, Clapham SW4 0BJ.).

You may find it worth joining the Country Landowners' Association (16 Belgrave Square, London SW1 8PQ; telephone 01-235 0511) even if you own no more than a garden, because this entitles you to free expert advice of various kinds (including legal and tax problems), discounts on insurance and some other things, a magazine about rural matters – with many advertisements for new or secondhand things of use to bed and breakfast owners – and various events. The CLA is as much interested in tourism as in other country activities: it publishes a useful book *Land: New Ways to Profit* (£5 to members, £6 to others) which covers this as well as other alternative enterprises which might be run in conjunction with bed and breakfast.

The Small Firms Service (government-run, and with a number of regional offices – simply dial 100 and ask for Free-fone 'Enterprise') is an advisory service available to anyone running, or thinking of running, their own business – bed and breakfast included. The service has information and contacts of every possible kind, and experienced business counsellors who give confidential, expert advice – up to three sessions free; for a fee thereafter. This could be very useful to anyone needing to make a full livelihood out of running a bed and breakfast or guest-house. All the big banks, too, are these days much more active in providing advice and help for small enterprises, and have departments devoted exclusively to their needs, now that there is much more money available for such purposes than there used to be.

Enterprise agencies give free advice about setting up small businesses, many employing only 2 or 3 people. The address of your nearest one can be obtained from Business in the Community, 227a City Road, London EC1 1LX (telephone 01-253 3716).

The Alliance of Small Firms and Self Employed People, 33 The Green, Calne, Wilts, SN11 8DJ, may be worth joining, especially for its varied bi-monthly newsletter, *Business Informer*. If you can join your local Women's Institute (they exist even in central London, not just the countryside), you will have access to much useful advice and information, including courses at their college in Buckinghamshire – some of which are on guest-house management and associated skills. Many W.I. members run bed and breakfast houses. Their publications cover subjects like cookery, curtain-making, lampshades, patchwork, picture-framing, upholstery, rush seating and other techniques. Details from the National Federation of Women's Institutes, 39 Eccleston Street, London SW1W 9NT.

Publications

Women's magazines have considerable resources of information and advice. For example, *Good Housekeeping* and its associated Institute run a free advisory service on cookery and domestic matters in the widest sense. For a fee (currently £20) they will do interior decoration schemes for rooms (see chapter 3).

The Consumers' Association is another good ally (membership details from PO Box 44, Hertford, SG14 1SH). It publishes *Which?* magazine, with impartial test reports on many of the things you need to buy, and also gardening supplements and an annual tax-saving guide (which cost extra). It also has a monthly bulletin on choosing wines. If you subscribe to its Personal Service you will receive help and advice when you cannot get redress for faulty goods or bad service. C.A. books include such useful titles as *Which Way to Buy, Sell or Move House* and *Starting your Own Business*.

You may find it useful to take a trade paper, such as *Caterer and Hotelkeeper*, weekly, even though much of its content relates to big business, because a number of the articles (and advertisements) will nevertheless contain useful information for you. It has an information service (telephone 01-661 3064) and also carries advertisements of bed and breakfast houses for sale and of catering equipment (new and secondhand).

Courses

To attend a short course on some aspect or other of your bed and breakfast work can be stimulating, not only because of what you learn but because of the exchange of experiences with other participants.

The Hotel and Catering Training Board runs a number of appropriate courses in different parts of the country (and has some home-study ones), for instance on the subject of starting up your own business. In their current programme are one-day courses on whether to set up this type of business or not – for people with no experience at all – with speakers that include experienced proprietors; two-day courses on how to set up your business – speakers include solicitors, accountants, etc.; and five-day courses for those already involved. A consultancy service at the HCTB headquarters costs, for an hour's advice, £40: and they publish such useful books as *Starting up your own Business* (specifically for very small hotels and the like) and a particularly useful *Small Business Information Pack* with details of helpful organisations, publications, sources of money, courses, advisory services, and specialist estate agents. For details write to the HCTB at International House, High Street, London W5 (telephone 01-579 2400). It has six regional offices too.

Local catering, technical and agricultural colleges sometimes run courses on subjects like farm or guest-house cookery, but check carefully what the syllabus comprises because it is disappointing to find yourself learning about very basic 'boarding house' food if what you want is a mini cordon bleu course. Other likely sources of information about local courses are adult education institutes.

The English Tourist Board 'Distance Learning Directory' has tourism courses that can be pursued at home. These include, for instance, one entitled 'Getting into Rural Tourism' which is run by Dyfed Open Tech in Wales. Home-study courses on starting your own business are run by the National Extension College (18 Brooklands Avenue, Cambridge, CB2 2HN) and the Open University (Box 76, Milton Keynes, MK7 6AN). The new Open College associated with Channel 4 television has short home-study courses on 'skills' subjects, including book-keeping and tourism: details from the National Distance Learning Centre, 527 Finchley Road, London NW3 7BG.

The City & Guilds Institute (46 Britannia Street, London WC1X 9RG) has added to its huge range of syllabuses one on guest-house management, and already part-time courses based on this (involving some 60 hours' study) are being run at about fifty colleges up and down the country. You can take one or all of its three parts: food preparation; food service and accommodation operations; customer contact and business aspects. The course is really intended for owners of guest-houses with, say, a dozen or more bedrooms to let, and many owners of bed and breakfast houses need something different – such as the type of very short course run at Hereford Technical College, which offers three-hour workshops on book-keeping, financial planning, taxation, and relevant laws (two workshops per subject); and two- to four-hour workshops on breakfasts, menu planning, vegetarian dishes, wine sales and afternoon teas (one workshop each).

The City & Guilds course deals extensively with health and safety aspects, and with basic cooking methods. It also covers choice of kitchen equipment, meal planning, purchase and storage of food, how to serve meals, cleaning, fuel supplies, plumbing and maintenance, choice and upkeep of furnishings, setting up and running a small business (including legal matters), marketing and publicity, administering reservations, book-keeping, costing.

146

It is worth bearing in mind that in some circumstances you can be paid an allowance for retraining – ask at Job Centres.

Writing in *Caterer and Hotelkeeper*, restaurateur Jean Barker said how much she, even though very experienced, had enjoyed a cookery course: 'The classes were small and the teacher and other mature students knowledgeable and interesting. We went through three or four skill areas each week, so we covered a tremendous number of dishes. All ingredients were included in the cost of the course, so we were able to bring home everything we made. My family soon learned to look forward to a gourmet tea each Thursday. I have really enjoyed the course and would recommend anyone in the trade to go on a similar one. It is surprising how much you forget or, worse still, the bad habits you acquire.'

Some of the courses in the general programme of evening classes which local education authorities run might be well worth attending: subjects are as diverse as flower arranging and first aid.

SUPPLIERS

From the Yellow Pages you will be able to discover the where-abouts of 'cash-and-carry' warehouses in your area, at which you are entitled to shop for bulk buys (and catering equipment) if you show your business card (or brochure). *Grocer* magazine publishes an annual directory of cash-and-carries and food trade organisations, and there is a directory of wholesale fruit and vegetable markets published by the National Federation of Fruit & Potato Trades; both are available in libraries. However, for many items you may get just as good prices at the nearest supermarket or hypermarket, so shop around. Ordinary shops, which may give you small discounts if you buy in quantity, should not be entirely bypassed. Local produce on your menu is a selling point, particularly if it is something out of the ordinary, like Cumberland sausage. Also, local shops will do favours for good customers, like displaying your card or letting you have onions at the back door on a Sunday afternoon! Women's

Institute markets are a good source of home-made cakes, preserves, etc. Bear in mind, however, the need to shop with dealers who give itemised receipts if you want to reclaim VAT (see chapter 9) on certain purchases.

Bulk buying with other bed and breakfast houses may help reduce the price, but don't overstock beyond your immediate needs; this ties up capital. Try buying direct from producers: eggs and vegetables from farmers, game and fish from sportsmen. Use your cheque book for purchases as this acts as a useful record. Where you do pay cash to suppliers, make sure they give you favourable terms.

Sources able to get you a range of goods at a discount include the following.

1 Country Gentlemen's Association – annual membership subscription (Icknield Way West, Letchworth, Herts).
2 British Federation of Hotel and Guest House Associations buying service (10 Green Lane, Ashwell, Herts; telephone 046 274 2633) for floor coverings, furniture, bedlinen, tableware, etc.
3 Your local hotel and guest-house association may have negotiated various discounts for its members.

When re-equipping a house, it is well worth visiting Kidderminster for its many carpet factories, Stoke-on-Trent and Worcester for china, Witney for blankets, Clitheroe for Sanderson's factory, or Bradford for Lister's velvet and other textiles, because you can there buy at factory prices: the local Tourist Information Centre will tell you where to go.

One bed and breakfast proprietor, who describes himself as a great explorer of trading estates, says that it is amazing what you find there. Mostly small businesses, often starting out and very willing to be helpful, they are often cheap. On one estate he found a good sign-writer, a man who was selling shop-marked electrical goods, and a textiles shop 'which has saved us a fortune'.

Mail order catalogues are particularly useful to people whose houses are distant from big shopping centres; and some mail order catalogues contain useful items not readily found elsewhere.

Do not despise secondhand purchases – except for such things as armchairs and mattresses with slack springs! Small advertisements in local papers, and in various magazines mentioned in this chapter, are a good source, as are auction rooms and *Exchange & Mart*. To dispose of surplus but serviceable furniture, remember it is not only saleable but often wanted by the Red Cross, Salvation Army, etc.

Finally, at the end of the book is a list of suppliers, many recommended to me by owners of houses in *Staying Off the Beaten Track* (for others, consult the Yellow Pages).

12.

Special-interest
Holidays

Sometimes it pays to offer visitors more than just accommodation, particularly at seasons when bookings are few. Also, doing something a bit different is a good way to get yourself publicity in newspapers and magazines – possibly national ones.

Your resources

The starting point when contemplating a special-interest holiday proposition is to consider what you might have to offer that is unusual or unique about:

yourself: have you a skill you could teach (riding, diving, one of.the almost countless crafts), a hobby you could share (collecting, nature study), or knowledge you could impart (local history, folklore, herbalism); and would you enjoy teaching or speaking on it?

your premises: have you a room big enough for talks by a speaker, a kitchen suitable for demonstrations, a modern milking parlour?

your possessions: goats, a grand piano, a minibus?

your locality: are you surrounded by prehistoric sites, stately homes, walking or climbing country; are there literary associations; are you near a theatre, or a cathedral where recitals are held, a forest or a bird sanctuary?

your acquaintances: do you know anyone who could teach, lecture, demonstrate, lead walks or tours?

your activities: beekeeping, farming, house restoration.

Thinking about such assets should inspire a few ideas. Next consider how involved you want to be and how much you could take on in addition to catering. Possibilities range from doing everything yourself, to arranging – largely a matter of organising other people – a package in which you provide the accommodation but the extras are someone else's function (whether arranged by you or already a going concern, like a theatre).

Involving others

If other people are involved, they must be both competent and dependable. While some professional speakers may expect a fee (or at least free accommodation), others may be glad to perform for nothing, particularly if it is in their own interest: a local wine merchant or antique dealer might give a talk on his or her subject in the expectation of attracting customers, for example. The WEA or a university extramural department might suggest speakers.

Many tourist attractions, such as mansions and visitor centres, will provide reduced-rate tickets, and they may agree to out-of-hours tours or talks for small parties (greatly preferable to seeing such places when they are busy). If you want to organise nothing more, you could at least try to get discounted tickets to offer to potential visitors as an inducement to stay with you. Block bookings for a play or concert are another possibility.

Concessions of this kind are most likely to be obtainable at the beginning or the end of the season, when an administrator has overheads to pay but patrons are few, and this is when you too are likely to want to boost bookings. *A Guide to Offpeak Marketing* (free) is worth getting from the British Tourist Authority, Thames Tower, London W6 9EL.

How complicated a package you arrange depends on how much of your own time you are prepared to risk in setting it up – money too, if you have to lay out any on such things as theatre tickets. At one extreme is one package that includes, as well as accommodation, a bus ride, a steamer trip, a slide show at a visitor centre, and a candlelit poetry reading with tea and local shortbread at a poet's birthplace. At the other extreme, one might simply let it be known that visitors can have a day out with a shepherd. (Such attractions, which require no particular preparation, are something else to put on your brochure – see chapter 7.) For some events, in order to ensure sufficient attendance to pay costs (e.g. a fee for a speaker), you may need to admit, if you have space, local day visitors.

Publicity

If a special-interest attraction is tied to a particular season or set dates, you will need to let people know about it well in advance through specialised magazines and so on (see chapter 7). You might also have a special card or leaflet printed to leave in all your rooms throughout the year.

As to other ways of publicising special-interest holidays, see chapter 7. In some ways the task is simpler than more generalised publicity because if you have a specialised subject to offer (such as angling or painting) you will be able to find your visitors through specialised magazines and clubs within the field concerned. One man left his career in industry and decided he would have to make his lovely home in 'Constable country' provide an income through bed and breakfast. He advertised painting holidays in the appropriate magazines. As a result the house is now virtually full for 30 weeks in the year.

Some possibilities

Buy the English Tourist Board's annual *Activity & Hobby Holidays* for ideas (and later you may want to advertise in it some special-interest holiday of your own). It includes holidays devoted to sports (from air to water), to crafts (from brass-rubbing to weaving), and to a host of other interests: amateur radio, antiques, astrology, chess, crime detection, driving, gardening, keep-fit, language and literature, philosophy, working with animals, etc.

Here are examples of what has been offered:

Week-long painting holidays;
Accompanied hill and moorland walks;
Wine tasting with an expert;
Tours of abandoned mines;
Brass-rubbing outings;
Bridge-playing;
Rough shooting or clay pigeon shooting in association with a
    local farm;
Antique hunting, with a shop trail and evening talks by local
    dealers;
Cookery weekends, including curry and cake-icing ones;
On farms, guided tours of the holding;
Elementary computer instruction;
Gourmet weekends (bed and breakfast at your house, top-
    flight restaurant bookings elsewhere);
Sea-angling or watching migrant birds (both at their best in
    winter);
Theatre and arts festival weekends;
Packages including sightseeing minibus tours;
On farms, demonstrations of working sheepdogs and cheese-
    making;
Landrover tours of a nature reserve;
Spinning and weaving lessons;
Glass-engraving tuition;
Tours of sites of hauntings.

The prize for ideas must go to a guest-house where they have offered watercolour tuition, recitals on the Northumbrian pipes, tours of Roman sites (the owner is a qualified guide), slide shows, meals based on Roman recipes, and helicopter trips – but not all at once!

Special occasions

Finally, if you were to let it be known (by a notice in each bedroom, perhaps) that, outside high season, you are willing to do weekend houseparties for families or friends at a reduced price, with special cakes for birthdays, Mothering Sunday, etc., you might get worthwhile return bookings just when you need them.

13.

The Role of Family and Employees in Health & Safety

In a small family enterprise, everyone – including any domestic helpers and older children – who may get involved should be aware of how to handle a telephone call or enquirer on the doorstep, how to make visitors feel welcome, what the charges are, where brochures are kept. No disagreements or crying babies should be overheard by visitors, no domestic or family crisis allowed to take precedence over the visitors' needs. If family and guests use the same bathroom, the family should not bath at hours of peak demand.

Teenagers in particular may find it irksome to refrain from disturbing visitors (with their record-players, for instance); on the other hand, some are very helpful and co-operative – even moving into a caravan for the summer while their bedroom is denuded of their possessions, to be let to visitors. Children may enjoy meeting other children who come to stay, or may resent seeing their swing or pets taken over. Some visitors like coming into kitchens: if you do not want this, conspicuous 'private' notices will be needed.

Daily routine

The work of a bed and breakfast house imposes on everyone a timetable that will restrict social life. Breakfast preparation may have to be done at 7.30 a.m. (sometimes earlier), with the morning taken up by washing the dishes, room cleaning, changing and laundering bedlinen, some preparatory work for

155

the evening meal, shopping and paperwork. Only the afternoon will be free (except for telephone calls) for a rest, bath or meeting friends. By teatime visitors will be coming in and the evening meal has to be prepared. Clearing up, having your own meal and laying breakfast-tables will keep you busy virtually until bedtime.

As to who does what when husband and wife together share the work, everything depends on their personalities and skills. One may like to be 'front of house', talking to guests; the other working behind scenes. One may like cooking while the other serves. Who is better at paperwork and accounts, at shopping, at gardening, at decoration . . . and so on? In no two partnerships will the answers be identical.

Hygiene

Any bed and breakfast house, however small, is as subject to the Food Hygiene Regulations as a big hotel. These are summed up in a free leaflet obtainable from local health authorities. They are enforced by local inspectors, some applying them more strictly than others. They have the right to inspect how bed and breakfast houses are run; and courts can fine offenders.

Before starting costly alterations to the kitchen, make sure that they will be approved. Examples of mistakes you might make are the following:

- Locating a washing-machine in the kitchen
- Failing to provide a separate basin for hand-washing exclusively, with soap, towel, nailbrush
- Choosing fancy kitchen fittings which harbour dirt and with surfaces which will not stand up to rigorous cleaning
- Having carpet or curtains in the kitchen

Other points worth noting are these. A pack of waterproof dressings (and burn dressings) should be kept in the kitchen for immediate use when a cut or burn occurs, the former being a common source of infection carried onto food. (The full first-aid kit which every house should have might also be kept in the kitchen.) Many foods present a risk of food poisoning if left around for long in a lukewarm state, which encourages germs to multiply – either keep them at over 63°C or put them in a refrigerator (this applies to every type of meat and fish dish, cream or imitation cream, cooked rice, and egg dishes such as custard and mayonnaise); thoroughly defrost poultry before cooking, never use the same cutlery or container for both cooked and raw meat (or pet food) – germs in the latter could be conveyed to the former; and never allow anyone to handle food who has a stomach upset, cold, boils, etc. Disposable paper is better than much-used cloths for cleaning up. It is best to serve sugar and preserves in covered bowls, to keep any flies away.

Neither dirty laundry nor pets should have a place in the food-preparation area (in one house, guests who objected to the sight of a cat eating a mouse in the dining-kitchen were told that only animal-lovers were welcome at the house: no one asked the mouse's opinion of this sentiment).

The hotel industry has been issued with guidelines to prevent the spread of AIDS. Points from it: do not handle discarded razor blades (or lend an electric shaver); wear disposable plastic gloves if any blood or vomit has to be cleaned up; and ensure the filters and chlorine supply in swimming pools, etc. are always working properly.

Visitors often comment appreciatively on the immaculate appearance of houses where they have enjoyed staying. Not only cleanliness but the look (and smell) of cleanliness create this impression: fresh paintwork, light colours, rooms aired by opening windows in the morning, and – instead of the smell of yesterday's cooking, cigarettes, dogs or even disinfectant – the scent of flowers, pot-pourri and furniture polish.

Safety precautions

Everyone involved should have some idea of what to do in an emergency, such as a burst pipe: where are the stopcocks, the fuse boxes, fire extinguishers, the list of emergency phone numbers (police, ambulance, water board, gas, electricity)? If your house is a rambling one in which guests might lose their way in a fire, family and staff should practise fire drill (the local fire service will advise): there is a useful booklet, *Act Quickly! Seconds Count!*, on what to do if fire breaks out, obtainable from the Hotel & Catering Training Board for £2.25 (International House, High Street, London W5 5OB).

With many people in a house, more than ordinary care is needed by family and staff to keep everything safe and sound, not least because a guest or employee injured as the result of (say) a loose stair-rod, a faulty electric appliance or a slippery floor might sue you (see chapter 9). The Health and Safety at Work Act 1974 covers not only employees. It requires you to ensure that your 'undertaking' is safe for all contractors, passers-by, and visitors too. Certain accidents may have to be reported to the Health and Safety Executive.

Many accidents (to which older people are particularly prone) are easily avoidable – for instance, by tacking down loose carpets, putting a white strip along a step that is not clearly visible, adding hand-grips where needed, leaving a landing light on during the night, choosing non-slip flooring for the bathroom and putting a non-slip mat in the bath. There should always be a clearly marked bell to your bedroom for use if an emergency occurs at night – something often overlooked.

Your own welfare

Finally, you and your own health. Bed and breakfast work can be strenuous – physically and emotionally demanding. When things are busy, you will be on the go from waking until bedtime with few breaks, and for seven days a week. It is essential to create time off, even if it is only an occasional day or two when you say 'no vacancies' to guests. Serving evening meals every night is a strain: some people tell their visitors that no dinner is served on, say, Wednesdays. Your own annual holiday will be limited to the slackest months of the year, which means that you will have to go far to get any sunshine. A major anxiety may be the fear of falling ill at a time when you have guests coming; and you need to have a contingency plan ready for such an event –

helpers who may rally round or, at the very worst, the possibility of finding alternative accommodation for the visitors. So building up a network of local contacts and support early on is very important for your own peace of mind, and so is a freezer supply of standby dishes ready to heat and serve.

It is one thing to start out with enthusiasm, energy and ambitious ideas (for instance, providing many choices at dinner, starched and ironed table linen, and so forth) but things which create a lot of work may overtax you in the end, particularly, as so often happens, when later extensions are added to accommodate more guests. Keeping life as uncomplicated as possible is not incompatible with giving your guests a good time.

Many bed and breakfast houses employ no help at all, until they discover how onerous much bedmaking and laundering is – this particularly applies when, say, an older couple take over a bed and breakfast house previously run by a younger family with several people sharing the work. There is something to be said for one spouse to have some part-time employment or paying hobby, so that income is not entirely dependent on bed and breakfast guests and so that paid help can be afforded.

Paid staff

It is probably best to employ nobody for more than about three hours a day, otherwise you will be lumbered with all the problems of their meals, tax, national insurance, employment laws (race and sex discrimination, hours of work, terms of dismissal), pension contributions and so forth, which come into operation once anybody works more than half time. In any case, such is the nature of bed and breakfast work that it lends itself to using part-timers, and these are often easier to find – housewives able to spare only a few hours a day are, for obvious reasons, very suitable, though mothers may not want to work during school holidays. If you live in a remote place, you may have to ferry them to and fro in a car, which is time-consuming. Another alternative is to employ a youngster full-time during the summer (a student waiting to start his or her course in the autumn, for instance – but check the national insurance position), if you have a room to spare – or a caravan tucked away in an obscure corner.

It is legal to employ children of 13 or more on household or garden tasks (but only for a couple of hours, and in the day-time). If Saturday is a peak day for changeovers, you might be glad of a young helper then.

Under the Youth Training Scheme, you may be able to get the services of a school-leaver for one or two years with the larger part of his or her pay borne by the scheme. This is on condition that you train the employee properly (you will have to set out on paper exactly what training you will give), and release them for some weeks in the year to go on a training course. A YTS overseer will call on you every few weeks to check on progress (there is form-filling to be done by you, too). Fuller details can be had from your local YTS.

To find an employee for this type of work, use Job Centres, careers offices, private employment agencies (these charge a fee), the local paper, and cards on newsagents' advertisements boards. It is better to telephone people whose names are given as references, rather than to correspond, for you are more likely to elicit a full and frank opinion this way. Recruit staff before the season starts so that you have time for training. At an inter-view, ask the applicants about their present work; describe the job you are offering – and invite questions. Tell them what the pay will be, also about hours, holidays and any possible snags; show them the house. Let them do most of the talking. Be sure you have the applicant's address and phone number, and know when they are available. Their first month should be on trial. When they start work, tell them the meal times and other routines; in explaining methods, frequently give the reason why. If you have explained everything clearly at the outset you will not need to keep supervising later.

Anyone who serves at table needs to be taught to hand dishes to the left of the visitor, to take dirties from the right, never to reach across, and to stack dirties tidily (first putting food waste into the waste bin). Be sure their clothes and personal hygiene (fingernails and hair in particular) are satisfactory, and brief them to answer questions like 'What is today's soup?' or 'What is Coronation Chicken?', and to spot guests' needs – for more toast, fresh coffee or whatever. You may get useful feedback from staff on whether guests are enjoying themselves or not.

It is impressive how often, in an owner's absence, a local girl or boy who comes in simply to help in the kitchen has very ably stood in for their employer – often conveying a real pride in and enthusiasm for the house and what it has to offer the visitor, which reflects very well on the way the owners have communicated their objectives to him or her, even if simply by example. It may be just as important to choose domestic helpers for their ability to get on with guests as for their cleaning or kitchen skills, particularly if they also serve at table.

Staff may receive tips (occasionally substantial), particularly if a box for these is put at the point where bills are paid; but in a bed and breakfast house these are the exception, and full wages should be paid regardless of anything else they may receive. If a visitor hands a sum to the host to distribute among staff where there is more than one person employed, it may be best to put this in a Post Office savings account (if they like this idea) for distribution, with interest, before Christmas.

The law relating to employees is rarely invoked where any domestic helper is concerned if he or she works few hours. Where others are concerned, it is worth getting a free booklet, *Employing People*, from one of the Small Firms Centres (e.g. 2 Ebury Bridge Road, London SW1; telephone 01-730 8451). Job Centres have a series of leaflets on topics like terms of employment, rights of expectant mothers, etc. Domestic workers in private houses are not covered by safety at work regulations, but the self-employed are, and so are workers in guest-houses: a leaflet on health and safety at work is obtainable from the Royal Society for the Prevention of Accidents (Cannon House, the Priory, Queensway, Birmingham, B4 6BS; telephone 021-200 2461).

14.
Doing It Yourself

If you are an experienced do-it-yourselfer, you will know your own skills and capabilities. If you are not, you would be unwise to learn on the job in a place intended for critical visitors. But it is important to be able to do running repairs. Such problems as blocked washbasins and broken windows are bound to occur and may have to be solved immediately or between the departure of one guest and the arrival of another. Getting professional help instantly may be impossible and is certainly expensive for such small jobs, so you will have to become adept at coping with small emergencies.

Major DIY is an excellent way of saving money, but only if you can achieve a professional result or better. It makes heavy demands on time and energy, which might be more usefully devoted to the direct welfare of your guests. So, apart from running repairs, it is an activity best confined to slack seasons or your annual closed period, when you will not have to attend to guests and keep work in progress out of sight.

What to tackle depends on your own abilities (though most people soon become adequately proficient in simple redecorating, one area where the saving over a professional job is marked). There are many guest-houses which have been lovingly refurbished to a very high standard by talented owners. But there are others where the rooms look as though they have been done over for a fiver one weekend. And there are houses which, uncompleted after years of struggle, have broken their owners' hearts, backs and bank balances.

What not to tackle

Apart from taking on too much for the time and money available, projects to be most wary of tackling yourself are:

1 those with a possibility of danger to yourself or your guests if you make a mistake, such as electrical installations;
2 those where you might injure yourself and thus not be able to look after your guests, such as roof repairs;
3 those where you might damage your property and contents if things go wrong, such as complicated plumbing;
4 those where official standards, which you might not know, have to be met: electrical installation again;
5 anywhere you might lay yourself open to a claim by an injured guest (who fell into a hole you had dug, for example);
6 anything which, if not completed on time, would reduce the comfort, safety or enjoyment your guests expect, or put any of your accommodation out of service at a busy period.

In addition, be wary of starting any work where the authorities are involved. If planning permission may be required, apply for it well ahead, especially if you are in a conservation area, national park, etc. (Planning officials are often very helpful informally.) Grants of any kind usually have to be sanctioned *before* any work is started. If a grant or Building Regulation approval is involved, you have to work to certain standards which may seem unreasonable. It might be more economic to do without the grant and work according to your own lights; but Building Regulations are legally enforceable (one householder had to rebuild an entire new staircase he had just finished, because the top step was half an inch too narrow).

Restoration work

The sort of work which is most rewarding in both senses is the painstaking refurbishment of what estate agents call 'period features' – the unearthing of old fireplaces, the restoration of fine plasterwork and joinery and the like. Much pernickety work of this kind would be impossible or impossibly expensive to have done by a builder; and the fact that owners have done such things themselves is of interest to visitors. (For their benefit as well as your own, it is worth taking photos before you start.)

The burden of DIY is greatly lightened if you can get casual help with the most laborious and heavy work – wallpaper stripping, cement mixing – leaving you to do the more interesting and responsible stages of the job.

Increasing your skills

You can, of course, increase your skills by studying books or going to evening classes. *Which?* is also worth an annual subscription. *The Home Improvement Price Guide* published by Spon tells how long various jobs should take, the skills and materials needed, and the likely cost. It warns that improvements rarely add to the value of a house anything like the cost of doing them.

15.

Bed and Breakfast on Farms

Bed and breakfast in farmhouses has increased in recent years: in some areas, so many farms now offer this that supply is perhaps beginning to exceed demand and no one should expect to have all their beds filled throughout the season.

In order to compete, some farms are adding more and more in the way of private bathrooms, swimming pools and games-rooms. These all have to be paid for and the cost passed on to the visitor, so the cautions expressed several times in this book apply. Consider, too, whether such added amenities are really in the spirit of a farm holiday, which is essentially homely, uncommercialised and cheap.

Special considerations

There are some particular pros and cons affecting farms. For instance, the need to look after bed and breakfast guests may be a nuisance when, say, lambing or harvesting needs the help of every adult in the family; visitors may not be keen on poor access and muddy yards, nor the smell (and flies) that go with cow-pats and silage; tenant farmers will need their landlord's permission (though he or she might even help with the cost of improvements or conversion of redundant farm buildings).

On the other hand, farms can offer special attractions for some visitors, not least children if there is livestock to look at, provided farm machinery does not create a hazard for them.

165

(The Health and Safety Executive, 1 Chepstow Place, London W2 4TF, has a leaflet on accident prevention for visitors to farms, and also material on children's safety.) They may be particularly suitable for people wanting to fish, shoot or hunt; and to accommodate field study groups. It is a good idea to give each visitor a sheet of typed notes (with plan) about what is to be seen on the farm, at each season – crops, stock, wildlife, farming practices and any necessary warnings about machinery, animals, etc.

Where farm produce can be used, good inexpensive meals can be provided at a profit, and many agricultural (as well as technical) colleges run catering and other courses in winter for farmers' wives. The very words 'farmhouse food' are an attraction to visitors weary of packaged products, particularly if regional specialities are on offer. Selling farm produce to take home is a profitable sideline. If yours is an organic farm, this will be a valuable selling point.

Incidentally, in the eyes of the Customs and Excise, bed and breakfast income cannot usually be separated from that of the farm as a whole and thus it may incur VAT even if it does not come to a large amount itself.

Added attractions

If you want to develop bed and breakfast trade in tandem with country pursuits to attract visitors to stay, consider the following options.

Fishing: you may have a suitable river or lake you can stock with fish, hiring out rods and boat if necessary, or land that could be flooded to make a lake (expert advice from the Ministry of Agriculture and your Water Authority should be sought). Non-residents could be charged a higher fee to fish.

Pony trekking: this needs to be well organised, so take the advice of pony trekking societies (there may be a course you could attend), and what you do will be subject to inspection by the local council. For advice on riding, consult the British Horse Society (National Equestrian Centre, Stoneleigh, near Kenilworth,

Warwickshire) unless all you intend to offer are short pony-rides on the farm grounds: ensure that BSI standard hard riding-hats are worn even for this.

Shooting is a highly specialised activity: consult the Game Conservancy (Fordingbridge, SP6 1EF: telephone 0425 52381).

Farm or nature trails: the Countryside Commission (John Dower House, Cheltenham, GL50 3RA; telephone 0242 521381) can advise on setting these up.

The Country Landowners' Association book, *Land: New Ways to Profit* (see chapter 10), contains guidelines for starting many new enterprises such as these, and others that could be tourist-related: water-based and other sports, pick-your-own and other ways to sell produce (including dairy products, jams and honey), deer farming and other kinds of 'alternative' livestock (even edible snails!).

Publicity

Farmhouse bed and breakfasts have their own publicity network. In most counties, there is a local group of about two dozen farms offering holidays, details of which are printed in one joint brochure. Usually inspection of the accommodation is a condition of joining in: some inspections are more rigorous than others. Details are obtainable from your regional Tourist Board or from the Farm Holiday Bureau. The latter publishes an annual directory of bed and breakfast farms, which is sold in bookshops (FHB Stoneleigh, Kenilworth, CV8 2LZ: telephone 0203 696969). The AA, British Tourist Authority, English Tourist Board and others all have farm holiday directories in which it is possible to advertise if your house conforms to given standards (see chapter 6).

Grants and advice

There are new ALURE (Alternative Land Uses and Rural Employment) grants to be had: 25% of the cost of providing tourist accommodation on farms, coupled with marketing advice. Details from Ministry of Agriculture. ADAS (the Agricultural Development and Advisory Service of the Ministry) has a socio-economic unit specifically concerned with promoting farm tourism and has a series of useful booklets.

16.

In Conclusion

Anyone who has read this far will have realised that to run anything more than the most limited bed and breakfast operation calls for a good deal of commitment. Yet hundreds who have chosen this way of life would not change if for any other. Typical comments by proprietors have included: 'I cannot think of a happier way to earn a living; our guests are a great delight to us – it is just like having a continual house-party except that they pay the bill when they leave!'; 'We ought to have become redundant years ago!'; 'Each guest has something different to offer. Perhaps my favourites are the single ladies who seem to have a great sense of humour and enjoyment, and the gentle retired couples with their special little requirements – it is nice to be able to spoil them a little'.

Most hosts sooner or later have experiences they treasure, such as the stay of a celebrated string quartet: 'After dinner we put the tables out of the way and they played for over an hour with the other guests as audience, and we tape-recorded it.'

Letters from visitors after they get home can be a joy and a reward to receive – like these examples.

Sent to Singleton Lodge (Lancashire): 'Your hospitality as hosts was not surpassed in our 5-week stay in England. We've had such fun telling family and friends of our stay with you – the trip to the barn to see the goslings – they should just about be ready for Christmas dinner – did the little lame one survive I wonder? As you can see by the pictures, I took an early morning walk and had a chance to see them swishing back and forth like melted butter. So dear people thank you for your part in our fantastic venture to your great country.'

Describing the Hare & Hounds (Cumbria): 'Joan and Les Stewart have an infectious enthusiasm for their work and attention to detail. Their manageress Mary delightfully "mothers" the guests and marshals the chores. The physical facility is nice and very comfortable. Admittedly, it does not reek of centuries of history, ancient stones or beams. What is it then? It is the *totality* of the experience and mostly it is *the staff* that makes your being there so very special! You feel as though you are "at home" with friends. Not only do you feel cozy and comfortable but you feel secure too. You will notice a "pub grub award" sitting on the mantel and your taste buds will affirm that too.'

and Highlow Hall (Derbyshire): 'For our Ruby Wedding celebration, our family journeyed from all parts. Mrs Wain and her family made us so welcome and did their utmost to make the occasion joyful and an unforgettable experience. A lovely thought of Mrs Wain's was to provide a large round table in the dining room to seat virtually all the family, and on the night of the celebration it was beautifully laid with ruby serviettes and centrepiece of gorgeous ruby fresh flowers. In fact we are planning our next celebration there.'

THIS is what it is all about!

Appendix 1.

After you have stayed at a few comparable establishments (and have yourself been operating for a while), try grading your house on the following scale.

		Below average	Average	Above average
Prices				
Quality of brochure				
Exterior:	house name			
	front drive or garden			
	parking space			
	paintwork etc.			
	absence of 'clutter'			
Entrance Hall:	appearance			
	cleanliness, tidiness			
	means of summoning attention			
Each bedroom:	appearance			
	cleanliness			
	lighting (esp. at bedhead)			
	adjustable heating			
	condition of beds			
	absence of noises			

	Below average	Average	Above average
Each bathroom: appearance			
cleanliness			
lighting			
heating			
ample hot water			
towels (sufficient, of good size)			
ventilation			
Dining room: appearance			
cleanliness, tidiness			
lighting			
heating			
staff: appearance, manner, efficiency			
Sitting-rooms, etc: appearance			
cleanliness, tidiness			
lighting			
heating			
condition of armchairs			
Breakfasts: quality, quantity			
varied choice			
Provision of tourist information			
Other amenities (TV, tea/coffee· facilities, etc.)			

Appendix 2.

Supplies, Services, Organisations

Most of the firms, organisations, etc., in the lists which follow have been included for one or more of the following reasons: they have been recommended by guest-house proprietors; they offer a postal service; discounts are available to bed and breakfast houses.

Bathroom

Bath re-enamelling
Phone 0270 626554

Shower cabinets
Dolphin Interiors, Bromwich Road, Worcester, WR2 4BD

Bathmats, etc, disposable paper
Chatsworth, 39 Waterloo Road, London NW2

Towel rails, hand-made
The Pine Co, 25 High St, Southampton

Drip racks, folding, to go over bath
Bowers, 01 903 0983

W.C. system, small bore
Transbyn, 62 Station Approach, South Ruislip, Middx

Shower screens
Specialist Factors, Box 14, Worthing, Sussex

Bedroom

Beds, folding, in cupboards
Golden Plan, 14 Golden Square, London W1R 3AG

Bedsteads, antique brass
Baddow Antique Centre, Gt Baddow, Chelmsford, Essex

Suitcase racks, folding
No. 1 Workshop, Red House Yard, Thornton Magna, Suffolk

Furniture
Stag Furniture, Nottingham

TV brackets
Pivotelli Broadaker Co Ltd, St Sampsons, Guernsey

Key tags, engraved brass
Timecourt, 61 Westgate, Guisborough, Cleveland

Mattress protectors
Abbey Quilting, Selinas Lane, Chadwell Heath, Essex

Financial, etc.

Insurance
Legal & General, Congregational & General, Avon, Norwich Union, Sun Alliance, Ecclesiastical (local offices); Bowring-Gauntlet (through membership of BHRCA)

Insurance brokers
Bernard Knope, Churchgate St, Bury St Edmunds, Suffolk
Cork Bays & Fisher, 10 Charterhouse Sq, London EC1M 6JS

Insurance, cancellation
Frizzell Bolton, 14 Elder St, London E1 6DF

Accountants
Griffin Stone Moscrop & Co, 41 Welbeck St, London W1

Property finding
Property Transfer, Claremont House, Second Ave, Hove, BN3 2LL

Book-keeping, postal course
Ideal Schools, Freepost, Woking, Surrey

Leasing equipment
Tudor Leasing Ltd, St John's St, Bury St Edmunds IP33 1SP

Flowers

Guy Wells, Whaplode, Spalding, Lincs

Guernsey Fresh Flowers, Le Couture Rd, Guernsey

Dried or silk
Rossetti, phone 01 587 3939

Food and Drink

Wines
Smedley Vintners, Rectory Cottage, Lilley, Luton, Beds

GM Vintners, 3 Alphinbrook Rd, Marsh Barton, Exeter, Devon

Majestic Wine Warehouses (branches)

Frozen foods
Beake Bros, Enterprise House, Godinton St, Ashford, Kent

Clotted cream
West End Dairy (Dorset), 0308 23203

Coffee and tea
Higgins, 01 629 3913

Algerian Coffee Stores, 01 437 2480

Gillards, Roast House, Weymouth St, Bath

Wild mushrooms etc
Fraiche of Edinburgh, 031 337 2969

Ham etc
Ashdown Smokers, 06578 324

Heal Farm 07695 2077

Haggis
McSweens, 031 229 1216

Herbs
The Herbary, 035 388 456

Chocolates
D N McVean, 41a Ilkley Rd, Otley, W Yorks

Cheeses
Wells Stores, Streatley, Reading, Berks

Smoked fish etc
Craster Kippers, Craster, Northumberland, phone 066 576 223

Brown & Forrest, 0458 251520

Pinneys of Scotland, 05763 401

Ritchies, 0700 3012

Loch Fyne Oysters, 04996 264

Unusual foodstuffs
Hale's Snails, 25 Pages Walk, London SE1 (and Manchester)

Kitchen

Freezer bags
Lakeland Plastics, Station Precinct, Windermere, Cumbria

Ironing machines
Fast Systems Ltd, 54 Friday St, Henley on Thames, Oxon

China and glass
Courtier, 267 Merton Rd, London SW18

Food processors, large
Robot Coupe, 60 Westbourne Grove, London W2

Coffeemakers, large
Cona, Railway Place, London SW19

Kitchen equipment shops:

Bath: Kitchens, Quiet Street. Rossiters, Broad Street

Belfast: Pattersons, Anne Street

Brighton: Chef's Larder, Chapel Road

Cambridge: Joshua Taylor, 6 Bridge Street

Cardiff: Allders. Queen Street

Cheltenham: Cheltenham Kitchener, 4 Queen's Circus

Chester: Romani, 9 Watergate Street. Lakeland Plastics, 11 Eastgate Row

Edinburgh: Studio 1, 71 Morningside Road and 10 Stafford Street. Wooden Spoon, 46 St. Stephen Street

Liverpool: Modern Kitchen Equipment, 2 Myrtle Street

London: General Trading Co., 144 Sloane Street. Elizabeth David, 46 Bourne Street, Westminster. Divertimenti, 139 Fulham Road and 68 Marylebone Lane. The French Kitchen, 42 Westbourne Grove. Covent Garden Kitchen Supplies, 3 Covent Garden Market. Jaeggi, 231 Tottenham Court Road and 124 Shaftesbury Avenue. David Mellor, 4 Sloane Square and 26 James Street (Covent Garden). Fairfax Kitchen, Swiss Cottage. Copper Shop, 48 Neal Street (Covent Garden). Hansens, 306 Fulham Road. William Page, 121 Shaftesbury Avenue. Staines, 15 Brewer Street

Manchester: Kitchen Gear, 65 Deansgate. David Mellor, 66 King Street

Newcastle on Tyne: Scobie Mackintosh, 46 Elswick Road. Cook's Corner, Leazes Arcade

Newcastle under Lyme: Homebakers, 157 Wolstanton High Street

Norwich: Quest, 1 All Saints Street. Jarrold's Department Store

Ripley (North Yorkshire): Tower Shop, The Castle

Southport: Modern Kitchen Co., 523 Lord Street

Staines: Jaeggi, 231 London Road

Swansea: Treasure, Newton Road, Oystermouth

Textiles

Household textiles
E Sunter Ltd, Wavel Works, Holcombe Rd, Helmshore, Rossendale, Lancs

Alexander Furnishings, 51 Wigmore St, London W1

HL Linen Bazaars, Churchbridge, Oldbury, Warley, W Midlands

Western Textiles, 10 Norfolk St, Colne, Lancs

Limericks, Southend on Sea, Essex

Furnishing fabrics, discount
Sue Foster, 11 High St, Emsworth, Hants

MSF, 194 Evington Rd, Leicester, LE2 1HN

Lilliput Textiles, Unit 90, St Michaels Trading Estate, Bridport, Dorset

Alexanders, 51 Wigmore Street, London W1 (telephone 01-935 7806)

Organisations

In addition to organisations and publications mentioned in the text, the following may be useful.

Bedding Federation, 251 Brompton Rd, London SW3

British Federation of Hotel, Guest House and Self Catering Associations, 5 Sandicroft Rd, Blackpool

British Hotels, Restaurants and Caterers Association, 40 Duke St, London W1M 6HR

British Carpet Manufacturers Association, 14 Pall Mall, London SW1

Corporation of Insurance & Financial Advertisers, 6 Leapdale Rd, Guildford, GU1 4JX

Arneway's Charity (for loans to start trading in the London area, for younger people particularly), 2 Greycoats Place, London SW1P 1SD

British Country Foods, 4 St Marys Place, Stamford, PE9 2DN

British Organic Farmers, 86 Colston Street, Bristol, BS1 5BB

Organic Farmers Ltd, Abacus House, Needham Market, IP6 8AT

British Contract Furnishing Association, Box 384, London N12

British Furniture Manufacturers Association, 30 Harcourt St, London W1

British Gas, 152 Grosvenor Rd, London SW1

Electricity Council, 30 Millbank, London SW1

Association of Independent Businesses, 108 West St, London SE1 3QB

British Institute of Management, Cottingham Road, Corby, NN17 1TT

National Chamber of Trade, Enterprise House, Henley on Thames, RG9 1TU

National Federation of Self Employed, 140 Lower Marsh, London SE1 7AE

Small Business Bureau, 32 Smith Square, London SW1P 3HH

Alliance of Small Firms and Self-Employed People, 33 The Green, Calne, SN11 8DJ

British Institute of Interior Design, Lenton Lodge, Wollaton Hall Drive, Nottingham

The Design Council, 28 Haymarket, London SW1Y 4SU

The Building Centre, Store St, London WC1E 7BT (and building centres in other cities)

Federation of Master Builders, 33 John St, London WC1N 2BB

Health & Safety Executive, 1 London Lane, London SE1 4PG

Catering Equipment Manufacturers Association, 14 Pall Mall, London SW1

Publicity

Picture postcards from photographs
Thought Factory, 40 Hastings Rd, Leicester

Interprint, Spa Lane, Harrogate (telephone 0423 889944)

Self adhesive photoprints
North Creake Photography, Royal Oak House, Fakenham, Norfolk

House signs, cast metal
Jacobs Forge, Freepost, Cardiff, CF1 1YW

Photographs from overhead
Cloud 9 (Southern) Ltd, Westbury Rd, Little Cheverell, Devizes, SN10 4JP

Post Office Direct Mail Dept
Room 195, 33 Grosvenor Place, London SW1X 1PX

Designer (brochures)
Kathy Gittins, Glamafon, Pontscowrhyd, Meifod, Powys

Miscellaneous

Upholstered furniture
Willis Workshops, Bodmin, Cornwall

Monotel (records cost of phone calls)
G H Smith Ltd, Colchester, Essex

Furnishing accessories, 'ethnic'
Traidcraft, Kingsway, Gateshead, NE11 0NE

Oxfam Trading, Banbury, Oxon

Maps and guidebooks for resale; registration forms
Explore Britain, Alston, Cumbria, CA9 3SL

Mail order goods
Scotcade, 33 High St, Bridgnorth, Shropshire (0274) 50175

Consultant on bed and breakfast
G.R. Sinclair, 27 Buchanan Drive, Glasgow G72 8BD

Architect (with experience of running a b&b)
Nicholas Hooper, Foxhill, Kingsey, Buckinghamshire HP17 8LZ (0844) 291650 (will give advice and recommend architects)

Solicitors (with experience of running b&b)
H. Howland, The Steppes, Ullingswick, Hereford HR1 3JG (0432) 820424

A Hackett-Jones, Pipps Ford, Needham Market, Suffolk IP6 8LS (044979) 208

Typing/word-processing services
Mrs A Christie, Hillards, Marsh Green, Edenbridge, Kent TN8 5PR (please telephone before sending work) (0732) 862404

Repairs and Renovation

Attic conversions
Velux, Freepost, Telford Rd, Glenrothes, KY7 4BR

Blinds, insulating
Anderson Window Insulation Ltd, 26 Store St, London WC1E 7BR

Staircase hand ropes
Outhwaites, Hawes, North Yorks

Plastic sheeting, etc
Transatlantic Plastics, Ventnor, IoW

Directory of repairers
Household Repairs and Replacements, Alifacts, Box 610, London SW7

Interior design, postal course
M Dwyer, 50 West St, Brighton, Sussex

Electric cable, switches, lighting fittings
CEL, Ullswater Crescent, Coulsdon, CR3 2HZ

Mailectric, Marsh Fold Lane, Bolton, BL1 4HH

Tools
J Simble & Sons, Queens Rd, Watford, WD1 2LD

Furniture fittings etc
Woodfit Ltd, Chorley, PR6 7EA

Chipboard Tables
Dormy House, Newton Park, Andover SP10 3SH

Some useful publications

Compact catering and other booklets on catering-scale equipment, free from the Electricity Council, 30 Millbank, London SW1P 4RD

Financing tourism projects, Tourism fact sheets (free), and *Tourism marketing for the small business* (£6), all from the English Tourist Board, Thames Tower, London W6 9EL

Food & Cookery Review, bimonthly from Rosaletta, 45 West Down, Gt Bookham, KT23 4LJ

In Business Now, bimonthly from Department of Trade, 11th Floor, Millbank Tower, London SW1 4QU

Promoting tourism to Britain: how BTA can help, free from British Tourist Authority, Thames Tower, London W6 9EL

Small Business Digest, free quarterly from National Westminster Bank, 3rd Floor, 116 Fenchurch St, London EC3M 5AN

Catering, free magazine from Dewberry, 161 Greenwich High Rd, London SE10

English Regional Tourist Boards

Cumbria Tourist Board
(covering the county of Cumbria)
Ashleigh, Holly Road, Windermere, Cumbria LA23 2AQ Tel: (096 62) 4444

Northumbria Tourist Board
(covering counties of Cleveland, Durham, Northumberland, Tyne & Wear)
Aykley Heads, Durham, County Durham DH1 5UX Tel: (0385) 46905

North West Tourist Board
(covering counties of Cheshire, Greater Manchester, Lancashire, Merseyside and the High Peak District of Derbyshire)
The Last Drop Village, Bromley Cross, Bolton, Lancashire BL7 9PZ Tel: (0204) 591511

Yorkshire & Humberside Tourist Board
(covering counties of North Yorkshire, South Yorkshire, West Yorkshire and Humberside)
312 Tadcaster Road, York, North Yorkshire YO2 2HF Tel: (0904) 707961

Heart of England Tourist Board
(covering counties of Gloucestershire, Hereford & Worcester, Shropshire, Staffordshire, Warwickshire and West Midlands)
2-4 Trinity Street, Worcester, WR1 2PW Tel: (0905) 613132

East Midlands Tourist Board
(covering counties of Derbyshire, Leicestershire, Lincolnshire, Northamptonshire and Nottinghamshire).
Exchequergate, Lincoln, Lincolnshire LN2 1PZ Tel: (0522) 31521

Thames & Chilterns Tourist Board
(covering counties of Oxfordshire, Berkshire, Bedfordshire, Buckinghamshire and Hertfordshire)
Mount House, Church Green, Witney, Oxfordshire Tel: (0993) 778800

East Anglia Tourist Board
(covering counties of Cambridgeshire, Essex, Norfolk and Suffolk)
Toppesfield Hall, Hadleigh, Suffolk IP7 5DN Tel: (0473) 822922

London Visitor & Convention Bureau
(covering Greater London Area)
26 Grosvenor Gardens, London SW1W 0DU Tel: 01-730 3450

West Country Tourist Board
(covering counties of Avon, Cornwall, Devon, Dorset, parts of Somerset, Wiltshire and Isles of Scilly)
Trinity Court, 37 Southernhay East, Exeter, Devon EX1 1QS Tel: (0392) 76351

Southern Tourist Board
(covering counties of Hampshire, Eastern and Northern Dorset and Isle of Wight)
Town Hall Centre, Leigh Road, Eastleigh, Hampshire SO5 4DE Tel: (0703) 616027

Isle of Wight Tourist Office
(Southern Tourist Board)
Quay Store, Town Quay, Newport, Isle of Wight PO30 2EF Tel: (0983) 524343

South East England Tourist Board
(covering counties of East Sussex, Kent, Surrey and West Sussex)
1 Warwick Park, Tunbridge Wells, Kent TN2 5TA Tel: (0892) 40766

Acknowledgement

We wish to thank Stephen Nicholls of Tor Haven Hotel, Devon for permission to reproduce the form on page 125.

Index